Debby Boone. Rita Coolidge. Olivia Newton-John. Linda Ronstadt. Stevie Nicks. Carly Simon. They're the SUPERWOMEN OF ROCK, the six most sensational female recording stars in the country!

They have all reached the top via different routes, but they all got there. Along the way there were plenty of struggles and hard work, laughter, love, tests of strength—and needed support from relatives and friends. But the most important thing they all share, these six very separate and distinct personalities, is a love for their music and for the entertainment and joy it brings to others.

Now here's the complete story behind six people you'll get to know intimately as the SUPER-WOMEN OF ROCK!

SUPERWOMEN OF ROCK

by Susan Katz

tempo
books
GROSSET & DUNLAP
A Filmways Company
Publishers • New York

Contents

A selection of photographs follows page 84.

SUPERWOMEN OF ROCK

Introduction

Not terribly long ago, women in the music world were ladies who made records in between having babies and cleaning house. No one, least of all themselves, took their career or their music very seriously.

In the forties and fifties, they were known as "girl singers," and more often than not they wound up marrying one of the guys in the band.

In the sixties, they were the ones to whom songs were dedicated, but there were no female Beatles or Rolling Stones.

It's all different now.

In the seventies, the reigning royalty on the music charts are women.

Debby Boone had the Number One solo recording longer that anyone in twenty-one years. She also won her Grammy over five male candidates.

Rita Coolidge, against all odds, came up with three gold singles from her first million-selling album.

Olivia Newton-John was the first pop singer to ever win the Country Music Association's Best Female Vocalist Award.

Linda Ronstadt is the first female rock singer to have five successive platinum albums.

Stevie Nicks exudes the same stage electricity that traditionally was possessed only by male rock singers.

Carly Simon is one of the reigning queens of rock, yet she hardly ever goes on tour.

In recent months, more than half of the top-selling

albums on the record charts have been made by women.

They have the world at their feet, these Superwomen of Rock; they have triumphed over what was a male-dominated industry and made it their own. They are clever, complicated, talented, and, above all, female. They have not sacrificed one bit of their femininity for their position on the charts, and that's what makes them all so very special.

1.
Debby Boone

When Debby Boone was sixteen she looked forward with great anticipation to her eighteenth birthday. Then she would tell her amazed parents that she was going to get a motorcycle and head for San Francisco, Flower Power, and a life of freedom from her strict upbringing.

It never did happen. And Debby isn't even sure now why she wanted to go, except that it was *Easy Rider* time, and she was feeling the pinch of parental restrictions and the need to cut loose.

"When you grow up in a family of four girls who look a lot alike and were dressed alike when we were younger, you want to be different. I rebelled against the whole family image for a while. I felt my mom and dad were overly strict and their values outdated. I thought, 'Wow, there's no help to be gotten from them. I'm going to have to figure out life for myself.'"

It's hard to imagine Debby, Pat Boone's daughter, as a rebel. She's so wholesome, so lovingly sincere, it's difficult to believe that the words "father knows best" were, at one time, enough to send Debby into an uncontrollable rage.

She was always a bit of an imp and a mischief-maker, even when she was just a toddler. Before she was old enough to go to school, she knew how to test her father's patience and tolerance. She approached him one day, sporting a wicked-looking black eye, and calmly told Pat that the little boy she had been playing with had given it to her. She was so cute and disarming that Pat

3

was amused rather than alarmed and got out his camera to preserve the moment for the family album. It wasn't until much later that he found out that he'd been had. Debby had been hit, but the shiner was her way of adding a little drama to a not terribly serious situation. She had painted it on. By the time Pat had discovered the truth, it was too late to do anything about it.

In time, Debby started to enjoy baiting her father. When she was fourteen and fifteen, she and Pat couldn't be in the same room together.

"If he tried to show me any affection, it made me crazy," Debby says today. "Also, being very much alike, we knew how to make each other angry."

Debby just couldn't understand why Pat was interfering with her life. It was embarrassing to have to turn down dates because neither she nor her sisters were allowed to go out until they were sixteen. All their friends were dating, but the Boone girls had to wait.

Perhaps their fiercest fight was over the artwork on Debby's side of the room she shared with her older sister, Lindy The sisters had agreed to each take one-half of the room and do what she pleased with it. Debby chose the kinds of "neat" posters her friends had—to Pat's eye, psychedelic and ugly. Pat begged her to change them: she refused, claiming they represented the essential Debby Boone. Pat took matters into his own hands and doctored them up with cartoons. She was so furious, she ripped everything down and locked herself in the bathroom, knowing Pat would be in an equal rage.

She was so angry, she couldn't see his hurt for her own. The breach between them lasted almost a year, and the healing process was a torturous one for them both.

"I don't think I ever want to go through with my kids what I put my parents through," Debby says. "They were just sick about me."

Today, Debby and her parents are closer than ever.

They share so many bonds, it's almost as if those dark years were all part of a bad dream. Even so, Debby is hardly a typical twenty-two year old, and all the events in her past have helped her to understand how to handle the extraordinary future that lies ahead of her.

Debby was born in Hackensack, New Jersey, in 1956. She was the third of four Boone daughters, all born within the first three and one-half years of Pat and Shirley's marriage. The whole family moved to Los Angeles in 1960.

Music was always a major influence in her life, and there was never any question of whether heredity or environment played the greater role in her development. She is the daughter of a singer and the granddaughter of one as well—country and western great Red Foley (Shirley's father). You might say there was music in her blood.

It's easy to guess that there was always some sort of singing going on with the Boones. Debby remembers songfests in the car going from one of Pat's tour dates to another. Church meant music, too, and the informal gatherings around the piano in the Boones' Beverly Hills home.

In those early years, though, Pat worked so much he was almost an absentee father. He was so very busy maintaining his status as the number one teen idol that his family was all but forgotten.

"When I was real young," remembers Debby, "he wasn't around very much. When he was there, he was a real good father. He just wasn't there enough. His marriage suffered for years. The family was kind of falling apart. He eventually worked things out. Performing and traveling with the family later was a way to keep it together."

When Pat and Shirley married, they were both nineteen. They had been going steady through high school in Nashville, when Pat was school president and Shirley was homecoming queen. He wanted to be a schoolteacher then, and the newlyweds moved to Texas so Pat could attend college, where he worked his way through by singing on TV and preaching guest sermons at a local church. The Boones and their first daughter, Cheryl, moved to New Jersey so Pat could finish up school at Columbia University in New York—he graduated cum laude.

Just after Debby was born, Charles Eugene Boone, better known as "Pat," recorded "Love Letters In The Sand"—it became one of his biggest hits, and he soon became the idol of millions of teenagers. With his white bucks and clean-cut all-American looks, he was every girl's dream man.

"You know, it's an odd thing," Pat remembers. "When I got started twenty-two years ago, my image and manner of life were normal, sort of middle of the road ones. And though there were rebels who were becoming popular then, too, I think I appealed to people who wanted to play by the rules and win, and I represented somebody who was doing that. For Elvis, it worked to break the rules and win, because he appealed to the rebel instinct."

Pat, Shirley, and the girls moved to California four years later, when things were changing radically. The clean-cut all-American-boy image that Pat and his white bucks epitomized was slowly but surely giving way to a new and far more rebellious type of hero. He had trouble maintaining his own beliefs, and finally he gave in. He lost a lot of his ideals and his music became a matter of compromise. He didn't much like what he was doing, even if it did sell records. He didn't much like himself either. He was like a chameleon, a different person for each new situation.

The backsliding eventually came to a roaring halt. "When we started traveling as a family act," Shirley relates, "show business, instead of a distraction, became the tool that kept us together. None of what happened to Pat will ever happen to Debby."

The whole family actually first sang together professionally in 1960, when Pat featured them on his TV show. But it wasn't until 1971 that Debby and her sisters, Cheryl, Lindy, and Laury—known as The Boone Girls—got their first big break. Pat agreed to take them on tour with him to Japan, where he was sharing the bill with another family group, the Osmonds. The deciding factor in whether the girls would perform or not was the song they chose to sing as a group. They came up with "What The World Needs Now Is Love," and the family act was launched. Dad and daughters played state fairs, hotels, amusement parks, and the musical circuits all over the world.

Debby's voice and seriousness about her music made her the natural leader of the girls. By the time she was fourteen she had already decided that her interest in a musical career was much more important than books and school, though she did graduate from Marymount High.

She wasn't much of a student anyway. Cheryl, the oldest, was the family's straight-A scholar; Debby didn't even come close. She blanked out on tests.

"I'd get nervous and forget everything I'd studied," she says. "Furthermore, I couldn't express myself well in essays so I'd put off writing them until the last minute and then I'd cry and want to run away because I couldn't even begin them, much less write the whole thing. So then Cheryl would help me."

On top of that, Debby believed her teachers didn't like her. She was never able to make friends with them like her sisters did, and if she complained at home, Pat would hightail it over to the school to find out what was wrong. This just compounded her misery, and she often suffered in silence, accepting D's rather than getting good grades "because Daddy talked with the teacher."

Debby went on to study at two Bible schools after high school. She spent a year and a half at one, studying the Old and New Testaments, and three months at a live-in school studying even further. She then spent about a year doing volunteer work with emotionally disturbed children, an enormous and loving undertaking. She became so involved and so sensitive to the problems of these kids that she considered going back to school to get a degree in special education. But her desire for a singing career was even stronger.

Of all the Boone girls Debby was always the different one. Cheryl had the brains; Lindy was most like her mother, quiet and gentle, and often the recipient of spankings for things that Debby actually had done; Laury was the athletic and adventurous one. Debby was so much like her dad it was scary.

She was the only one of the four who wanted to pick out her own clothes and lighten her hair—an experiment that failed. She wound up with a mop of bright orange frizz that took months of reconditioning to undo. But she's not sorry she was the one to break out of the mold to become the only sister really interested in a singing career. She says she was always a rebellious child, the one who "sassed back." And the frequent clashes between her and Pat could be over anything, even her health.

Debby was a coffee drinker, almost addicted to it. Pat's strongest stimulant is milk—he still drinks a quart of it a day. He tried to warn Debby about the ill effects too much coffee would have on her system, but she wouldn't pay attention to him.

"My father is very health conscious," she explains. "He tried to discourage me from drinking coffee. It was silly, of course, but the more he criticized me, the more coffee I drank. One day I had the shakes, and my doctor told me it was from my caffeine addiction."

Then she listened. Her eating habits were so bad that she had almost no energy. A nutritionist helped put her back on the road to good health with a plan to rid her system of all the toxic elements she had put into it. The program included two days of raw apple juice and spring water, followed by the addition of protein with chicken and fish. But since the goal was to clean her system out, she could not have vegetables and fruit at the same meal. It's not a program Debby suggests anyone try on their own, only under the supervision of a knowledgeable expert in the field, but she says she feels great now. She's off sugar and white flour, and whatever sweets she does eat usually have raisins as their prime ingredient.

Luckily for Debby, she doesn't really have to diet. Her weight has always been pretty constant, and her true test of whether she's gained or lost weight is how she feels in her clothes, not what the scales show. It almost made her a little uncomfortable to see how depressed her sisters would get every time they stepped on the scales, so she doesn't even bother with one.

Once again, father did know best, and Debby found it out the hard way. But it's all a part of growing up.

Her feisty nature also rebelled somewhat against the extensive religious training her parents insisted on giving all the girls. It started when she was very young. Pat always felt that religious work with young people was very important and he made no exception for his own children.

"I don't feel I was ever indoctrinated," Debby says. "But there was a time, between the ages of fourteen and seventeen, when I started developing my individuality and feeling alienated.

"I went through a really bad period of doubting. I

wasn't sure whether my beliefs were my own or something that had been forced on me. And I was really struggling to be an individual."

It's not that she could only do certain things—rules are invented to be circumvented—but her own choices left her wondering whether she would be left out of the mainstream if she took a firm stand.

Pat proudly tells interviewers that his girls were not always chomping at the bit to get out from under his strict tenets and rules, although he does admit they've had their differences of opinion.

He remembers Merv Griffen asking his daughters whether they were missing out on life because their parents were so strict. Cheryl answered for all of them: "I'll tell you what we're missing out on—trouble." Pat couldn't have said it better.

And he was also proud of Debby's response to Johnny Carson when he asked her if Pat was still approving all her dates. Debby simply smiled and told Johnny: "I'm much more particular than he is." It managed to leave Johnny Carson speechless and Pat laughing with delight.

Pat still keeps a rather watchful eye on his girls, even though Cheryl is married to religious publishing executive Dan O'Neill, and Lindy is the wife of record producer Doug Corbin. They still get Pop's usual good-bye whenever they leave the house, "B.P. and C."—"Be prayerful and careful." When Lindy had her first daughter, Jessica, in March 1978, Pat was right there in the delivery room with Doug and the medical staff of the hospital. He was leaving nothing to chance. Both Cheryl and Lindy have given up their careers for motherhood and missionary work, although they do appear on Debby's album, singing background vocals, and have appeared with the rest of the family on the Boone TV specials.

When Debby won her Grammy Award, it was delivered to her dad, who brought it home to her. And all her dates must pass his inspection as well as hers. Laury is a student at Pepperdine University and is only around on weekends. She manages to escape her eagle-eyed father most of the time, but she's still subject to his watchfulness when she's at home.

Living at home suits Debby, though, at least for now. She can't see doing it forever, and naturally she'd like to be able to see what it's like to live alone before settling down and getting married. Pat, of course, doesn't feel that that is the best thing for her. He lived at home until he got married and feels he didn't miss out on anything.

"For now," Debby says comfortably, "it's working out well. It's a stabilizing factor. I did a show with John Denver in Australia a while back, and I had to stay in a hotel room by myself for two weeks. I really missed my family. They help me keep things in perspective.

"I've seen a lot of people in the entertainment business get very confused and feel paranoid and used. I think I'm avoiding problems like that by living at home."

It's very difficult for a young person, suddenly the hottest singing sensation in the country, to keep herself and who she is in the right perspective. When people are constantly making a fuss over who you are and what you're doing, it's nice to have an understanding and welcoming family to go home to. It's a warm and gentle reminder of just who you really are. A family like Debby's just won't accept any phony stuff from her; she's the same to them—and hopefully to herself—as she was before "You Light Up My Life" lit up her life.

Pat and Shirley have no arguments with Debby's philosophy. She has almost total freedom; they trust her, and there's really no need for them to set any restrictions.

"Having a home, a family to come home to, that's a wonderful thing," Pat says. "I'm forty-three and I love going to visit my parents back in Nashville and letting Mama cook for me. But I know what Deb's saying. She knows she could move out and take on some extra responsibilities, but . . ."

Debby has no curfew, although Pat and Shirley once tried to convince all their daughters that there was absolutely no reason for them ever to be out after midnight. It didn't work. Of course, Debby always tells her folks where she's going and with whom, so there's not much cause for worry.

"Besides," Debby says, "a wild social life doesn't suit me. It's more fun staying home. I don't go to parties much. Even in high school I didn't go to many dances. I've never really enjoyed drinking much. I don't smoke or drink, but I do have a glass of wine occasionally. That's really daring for me."

Most of her friends are musicians or connected to the music business in some way or another. Shaun Cassidy and Gina Martin (Dean's daughter) are among her closest friends; Donna Freburg (daughter of humorist Stan) and Gabriel Ferrer (son of José Ferrer and Rosemary Clooney) are also constant companions.

But even more important to Debby than lots of dates and a swinging social schedule is her spiritual life. Her values are strongly entrenched in her way of life. Pat and Shirley have never made any secret of their religious beliefs. And Debby, while perhaps not as preachy about them as her parents, doesn't for a moment let her Christian heritage leave her.

Debby is totally satisfied with herself. If some folks prefer to believe that she's sheltered, naive, and innocent because of the way she's been brought up, that's fine with her. To a great extent it's true and certainly nothing to be ashamed of. She just doesn't feel she has to know *everything* that's going on—especially the "smutty" negative things, as she calls them. What's the point, she wants to know, if it doesn't benefit her life to know they exist?

"A lot of people figure we're not for real," she laughs. "They figure we couldn't be happy, that we're just sticking this out because of some sort of indoctrination or that we're not telling the whole truth. But we are real happy and we do live the way we say. I think maybe people who can't accept it are people who aren't living up to their own standards."

She's straightlaced by choice—she lives at home because she wants to, goes to church because she wants to. It's important to her because she has made her own choices.

"I guess I'm rather old-fashioned in my standards and beliefs. My life would have probably been very acceptable in the time that my father was famous. Now I'm the one who stands out like a sore thumb."

Pat's rather comfortable with that. In his eyes his daughter is a true rebel, however ironic that may seem.

"She's going against the grain," he says with a touch of pride. "I think people will respect her for her independence. When I got started, my ways weren't very unusual. I was thought of as an old stick in the mud, representing an idea that was becoming passé.

"With Debby, the idea's almost new again. For a young person to have her kind of convictions is unusual and different. So I think maybe people are more apt to respond to her positively than they ever did to me."

The response to Debby has been nothing short of phenomenal.

"You Light Up My Life" was her first solo effort and it sold more than four million records. The biggest single of 1977 and of the past twenty years, "You Light Up My Life" won Debby a Grammy Award as the Best New Artist of the Year. (The song was also awarded an Oscar as the Best Song of 1977.)

Debby was totally unprepared for the storm that followed the release of the record. The year hadn't started off spectacularly for her at all. From January until September of 1977 Debby pretty much just hung around, traveled with the family, went to a gym to work out, met friends. She wasn't happy with all this free time, but she hadn't yet found the right songs to record.

Enter Joseph Brooks, writer, producer, and director of a low-budget moved called *Sessions* about a young girl who writes songs and wants to become a singing star. She lives in Los Angeles with her father, is engaged to a tennis teacher, and gets her big break when a film director leads her to believe he's interested in using her song in his movie.

But Joseph Brooks couldn't sell his movie to anyone. None of the major studios were interested in it because it had no stars. The recording companies weren't interested in the sound-track, which Brooks had also written. Finally Columbia seemed to show some interest, even though they weren't sure how they could market a movie that featured virtual unknowns.

"Leave it to me," Brooks told Columbia. He says now: "I knew it would be a hit. There's a void of films for teenagers, but this film appeals to everyone. The point of the movie is that you can be what you want to be, but you can only depend on yourself. That's an important message for teenagers."

Brooks made the music the star of his film by changing its title to *You Light Up My Life*.

There are two albums called *You Light Up My Life*. One is the original sound track from the movie, with the title song by Kacey Sisyk who dubbed the movie version for actress Didi Cohn. The other—with the hit single—is Debby's.

The film does not credit Kacey with the singing, and there is still a legal battle raging as to whether Brooks did her out of what is rightfully hers—royalties from the sound track.

So where does Debby come into the picture? Brooks had invited Mike Curb, president of Warner-Curb Records, to a special screening of *You Light Up My Life*. Debby had been under contract to Curb for several years, and he had been looking for a single to help her solo career take off. The film was about to be released, and Brooks needed the single fast—despite the fact that he didn't have the money to rerecord the song's orchestral track. Fortunately for everybody, except maybe Kacey, Debby and Kacey sing in the same key, so rerecording wasn't necessary. Brooks produced the single well within his time and money limits.

In just seven weeks Debby's version was Number One. Both albums, Debby's and the sound track, have sold millions of copies, and nearly every one is happy.

Kacey still feels she should have been given credit in both the film and the album at the very least, and Debby is a bit upset that some people are confused enough to buy the sound track thinking she's singing on it. She doesn't feel it really hurt her album's sales any, but she'd like to set the record straight. Nor does Debby have any qualms over being the one with the smash single.

Debby didn't even see the film until her record had already hit the top of the charts, although she did hear the sound track before her own recording date.

She wasn't totally pleased with her album, although she thinks the single is spectacular.

"I don't feel like I was tested on the album," says Debby honestly. "Because of the rush of it, a lot of compromising had to be done on my part. In the future I hope to have more to say about material. I want to be involved in the concept stage right through to the mixing."

Some of the compromises involved adding some old

material to make up the balance of the album, stuff from earlier sessions, which no one had been all that pleased with. But the album was well received critically, and her style has been called gentle, intimate, and warm. The critics have pointed out her feel for ballads and her sparkle on songs that are more rock numbers.

"Each week the song was Number One I had mixed emotions," Debby confesses. "I'd get excited, of course, but I'd get a little frightened too.

"I'd worry, what am I going to do next? Now I've realized that I'll just keep doing what I did before. I didn't struggle and strive thinking 'How can I get a Big Hit?' I just looked for songs and then recorded them. So that's what I'm going to keep on doing and see what happens."

Neither she nor her dad think she'll come up with another whopper like "You Light Up My Life," but Debby's sure that people will realize that the song was not an easy one to sing and that she had to have some talent to sing it that well.

"I think people will probably figure out that whatever I do next will be a good record too. At any rate, I just can't worry about it anymore."

What Debby does worry about is her future in general. She started to take some singing lessons to improve and build her voice, but she felt they were making her lose her spontaneity. She's thinking about acting lessons, too, so she can seriously consider some of the film offers that have come her way. But one thing she does know for sure and that is that she'll always want to sing.

The out-of-town promotional tours, the interviews, the album-signing sessions, and the people who came up to her to tell her that they couldn't get her song out of their minds or that their grandchildren knew all the words, made Debby feel so good and so committed to proving she's not just a one-album wonder but a lasting talent. Her second album was released in late spring, and her biggest decision now is whether to commit herself to a family TV show for the fall. She's not sure about that, although the pressures from Pat are rather great. But among other things Debby's learning to say no, and her ultimate decision about this will be her own.

Debby's instant success has spurred Pat into taking the kind of action he's been neglecting over the past several years. He hasn't had a hit record in years, and he's glad that Debby's inspiring him to do more.

"Debby is challenging me," he says. "I can't get sloppy when she's around, and I am singing better than I have in a long time."

But there's no real competition, just a healthy give-and-take. Debby thinks that if she had been a boy, there would definitely have been some fierce competition between them, but Debby and Pat have limited their rivalry to who can hold a note longer.

"I'm beginning to feel a little like Norman Main in *A Star Is Born,* but I'm not ready to take a walk into the ocean," laughs Pat.

Pat feels quite strongly that the music business today, especially in the rock area, has become tough; in his view rock has been invaded by the baser elements in the business and is not really entertainment anymore. So it's sort of natural that he worries about Debby and her exposure to this kind of influence. But he feels that she can handle it, and he's absolutely confident that his guidance will keep her from going astray. He thinks she's easily as good a singer as Olivia Newton-John or Barbra Streisand, and although his first reaction when he heard that "You Light Up My Life" had gone to Number One was to take a four-hour walk to digest it all, he couldn't be happier for Debby.

When his good friend Perry Como called Pat to tell him he had seen Debby on TV and thought she was terrific, Perry asked whether Pat was even just the least bit jealous.

"Not at all," said Pat. He explains: "It's a funny thing but when one of your children does something, you not only vicariously experience it yourself, especially if it's something you've already done, but there's a little bit of an extra dimension that's hard to explain."

Pat doesn't hesitate to point out that Debby's record has not only surpassed any single by a female in the whole rock era but also his own biggest hit as well, "Love Letters In The Sand," which was Number One for six weeks in 1956. He's as proud as if he had done it himself. "You Light Up My Life" has topped every other single released in the past twenty years, including hits by Elvis and the Beatles. The only record it hasn't vanquished, Pat says, is Perez Prado's 1955 hit, "Cherry Pink And Apple Blossom White."

Debby's newfound stardom is having a noticeable effect on the entire Boone family. Their Beverly Hills home, which has always been indicated on the find-the-stars'-homes maps, is suddenly surrounded by electronic gates to keep out the hoards of fans who want to meet Debby. She has had to get a full-time secretary to answer her fan mail. All four of the sisters are sharing in the profits from the album sales, since they all sang on one song or another. That, in particular, has strengthened her relationship with the family to the greatest extent.

After "You Light Up My Life" Debby had a minor success with her follow-up single "God Knows." Now "in the can" is the title track from Brooks' new film, *Hollywood* and the sound track album for the upcoming *Magic of Lassie*. Debby and Pat have been booked into Las Vegas's Sahara Hotel, reportedly at a fee that is a great deal higher than what even their individual fees would add up to.

Perhaps Debby's biggest project these days is writing songs for Pat's Lamb and Lion religious label. Several artists are under contract, but it hasn't been doing terribly well. Distribution problems seem to be the chief cause.

"Commercial people tell us we're too religious for them," Pat explains. "And the religious ones tell us we're too commercial. But I think this music could sell if given a chance. I think a lot of young folks will listen to it."

Maybe with Debby contributing some of the music it'll have a better chance. After all, she has said many times that "You Light Up My Life" was recorded while she was thinking about God.

"I knew when I first heard the song that it was probably written in the context of a guy-girl relationship, but I hadn't seen the movie then and for me it lent itself to these spiritual feelings.

"So whenever people ask me if I was singing it about a special person, I can't really say yes because I was really singing it about God."

Despite her religious bent in that particular song, Debby gets totally involved in things like arrangements and recording techniques when she's cutting a record. Pat used to just walk into the studio and have someone play him the dub of the song he was going to do.

"Then I'd rehearse for half an hour and record it in one or two tapings," he says. "I'd let it all hang out. Go for broke. I got at least ten gold records that way. Maybe in some ways it was irresponsible, but it worked for me."

It sure did. No matter what shortcuts he was taking musically or what compromises he was making personally, he was always, to his adoring public, perfect, the very essence of romance.

Debby takes after him in that respect. All his daughters do, but Debby is the most public about it. You know their past frictions have been totally forgotten when she says, "I want to thank my father for this image. It's a straight image, a square image, a strong image. It's been a built-in protection for me. It's like a big protective shield that helps keep out the ugly things in life."

She has a superclean wholesomeness that makes people want to see if they can shock her silly by swearing or talking about something they know she's uncomfortable with. But her straightness doesn't mean she doesn't like to have fun. She does. Fun to her means being with good friends, playing tennis, horseback riding, and sailing. Good clean fun.

"I know a lot of people tend to think of me or paint me as sort of a sheltered, naive, sweet innocent. Some of that is true.

"But I'm not real naive. Everyone is sheltered in some way or another. And I do resent it when people think that just because a person is wholesome and kind of spiritual they're outdated and boring and unintelligent."

Her attitude is most definitely reflected in the kind of men she dates. She'd never think of going out with anyone who didn't think the same way she does—it just wouldn't work. The pressures would be far too destructive to a relationship.

"I guess," Debby says, "I've just never found it that hard to stick to my standards. I don't know what to attribute it to except maybe help from God and only getting involved with people who feel the same way I do.

"Besides," she goes on. "I'm not the kind of girl who's always looking for guys to date anyway. I don't worry about trying to establish a heavy relationship. I figure, when the time is right, it'll all happen naturally, and until then I'm not going to sweat it." She's already the "old maid" in the family, but who cares?

When Debby finds Mr. Right, he will be someone who is very honest, secure in himself, and strong—and someone whom she feels God has chosen for her. He will, naturally, have the same high moral and personal standards she does.

What it all boils down to, and what Debby admits herself, is that she'd never settle for a man who had less than all the good things she respects and loves in her father. And there are many things that she really does love and respect.

Among those qualities are Pat's concern with good health and physical fitness and his cool, calm way of facing up to problems and stumbling blocks—he just does not get upset easily, lose his temper, or get nervous. "He always seems so collected," Debby says, "and I have a tendency to panic, so I respect that in him."

Pat's sense of humor is another quality Debby admires. He's an easy person to laugh with, and it wouldn't be possible for Debby to spend time with someone who didn't like to laugh.

"But," the philosophical Ms. Boone says, "you never really know what you're looking for until you find it.

"You think of all the things you like, but when it happens—when you fall in love with someone—there will be things you never thought you were looking for."

Not that Debby's in love, thinking of getting married, or even dating anyone seriously right now—except maybe for Gabriel Ferrer, who's as much of a close friend as he is a date. She's had a few long-term serious male friends in the past, but she really doesn't like the whole dating game. The possibility of her not getting married doesn't frighten her, although she does want to have kids before she's too old to enjoy them. In any case, she doesn't see it happening anytime soon. She's not running away from it, but she's not actively seeking it out either.

Her attitude is directly opposite to her father's. Pat tends to think that Debby and the rest of the girls will be more fulfilled as wives and mothers than as career women—singing should be their secondary goal, family the primary one.

Debby's not so sure of that. She feels that her career,

at least now, is very important, far more important than thinking about raising a family.

Pat knows that his daughters can ultimately take care of themselves and that their decisions will be the right ones for them. Their years of spiritual training will support and protect them, no matter what paths they should choose to follow.

But still, he is most concerned about Debby and how she is going to maintain her image in the hard-boiled world of the music industry. His own experiences have proved that it isn't always easy.

Debby is not worried.

"I have to follow this through," she says. "I'll watch the compromises. I want to keep my ideals and my musical integrity. Before I make too many crucial compromises, I'll quit the business. If this business is so twisted that I have to change my values to work in it, then it's really no place for me."

That's her father's daughter speaking.

"She's twenty-two and she knows just who she is," Pat Boone says. "Debby has to do what I did: adjust and make it work anyway. I'm just glad to be along for the ride."

DISCOGRAPHY

Debby Boone   *You Light Up My Life,* Warner-Curb
                Records BS 3118
                Midstream, Warner-Curb Records
                BSK 3130

2.
Rita Coolidge

Rita Coolidge might just be one of the most envied women in the world.

She's got a career that has made her the international star she deserves to be; a voice that soars and dips with incredible range; a face and figure that can only be described as strikingly beautiful; an adorable, intelligent, and loving four-year-old daughter; and one of the handsomest, sexiest, and most talented husbands to ever hit the movies, Kris Kristofferson.

And she is, not surprisingly, deliriously happy.

The daughter of a Baptist minister, born in Nashville, Rita began her singing career when she was just two years old. Her father stood her up in the front row of the church choir and said, "Sing." Thirty years later she's still at it. You can still hear an element of that rich gospel influence when she sings, a quality that has made some critics call her the best blues singer since Janis Joplin. Others compare her firm, controlled voice to Bonnie Bramlett and Tina Turner.

Rita put her voice to work for her in college, singing on weekends to pay her way through Florida State University where she earned a teaching degree. She was never going to make a career of it. After she graduated she couldn't find a job, so she started singing again while she worked toward a master's degree in fine arts. She was very soon off campus and on her way to singing professionally.

"I thought I'd work for a year," she says in her casual

way, "but at the end of it I was hooked."

She went to Memphis and was lucky enough to land a job doing background vocals on commercials. In that soulful city she cut her first single, "Turn Around And Love Me." It became a smash hit locally, but Rita was already somewhere else.

It seemed as if everything started happening at once. As "Turn Around And Love Me" became an overnight sensation in the South, Rita flew to Los Angeles to join Delaney & Bonnie & Friends on their national tour and sang on their now-classic album, *Accept No Substitutes*. The record's producer, David Anderle, who has produced all of Rita's records, claims he knew then that Rita's sultry sound was going to be big and that he would be the one to get her voice on a record.

"I knew it would be a while before it would happen," he said. "The years, maturity, and increased confidence in her womanhood have allowed Rita this expression, and it's as good as I dreamed it would be."

From Delaney & Bonnie Rita joined up with Joe Cocker's Mad Dogs and Englishmen. It was an experience that literally changed her life. She was introduced as a solo artist during the worldwide tour that was to become notorious for its wild, frenetic craziness.

The Mad Dogs tour was worth it all in the end. Not only did people see the dark-haired vibrant lady up on stage, they also listened. She was building her reputation as a performer.

During this time Rita was also contributing backup vocals to albums by some of rock's most prestigious artists: Dave Mason, Graham Nash, Eric Clapton, Stephen Sills, and Booker T. Jones (who later married Rita's sister, Priscilla). Leon Russell was so taken with Rita he dedicated his beautiful "Delta Lady" to her. Her name and voice were becoming so respected and admired that when she recorded her first album for A&M Records, *Rita Coolidge*, many of these same artists rallied round to lend their voices.

That was in 1971, the same year Rita met Kris Kristofferson. The electricity between them was immediately apparent from the moment they first set eyes on each other in the Los Angeles airport. Yet, according to Kris, that meeting almost didn't happen.

"I'd just broken up with this girl, felt really funky," he recalls. "I was on the way to Nashville to do my first interview with *Life* magazine and Rita's manager recognized me.

"I was in no mood to deal with anybody, but when people recognize you, you gotta deal; it's one of the prices you pay. He introduced Rita. She looked . . . well, she looked like something else. On the plane they saved a seat for me."

Rita says she knew from that very first minute that she would be with him forever.

"By the time we'd been together for a day, we'd already named our first child Casey," says Rita

The thing that impressed Kris the most during that plane ride was that Rita really listened, was really interested in what he was saying. So instead of staying on the plane to Nashville to meet the reporter from *Life* he got off with Rita in Memphis where she was meeting her band to go off on a road tour. He never did get to do the *Life* interview.

"My next booking was in Edmonton," Kris says. "So was hers, except that somehow hers got cancelled. I said why not go with me, and we've been booking out together ever since."

Rita's cancellation, as fortuitous as it may have been for romance, was just one of her many disappointments during that tour. She was finding out the hard way just how difficult it is for a performer to make it on the road. Her reviews ranged from the ecstatic ("she should be heard") to the unenthusiastic ("bland and plodding").

"The truth is," Rita admits now, "I was bombing out

when I met Kris. I was having shows cancelled for lack of ticket sales, and I was heavily in debt because of trying to keep the band out on the road.

"Working with Kris was good for both of us. It gave him some time off during the show, and it exposed me to more people. Before that I had a deep lingering fear of someday not being able to make any more records."

Kris was at the very peak of his popularity. He was the golden boy who could do no wrong, and Rita would learn more from touring with Kris than she could ever hope to on her own.

They were married in 1973, and their daughter, sure enough named Casey, was born a year later. They toured together, recorded together (*Full Moon* for A&M, and *Breakaway* for Kris's label, Monument), and even made a film together, *Pat Garret and Billy the Kid*. Kris was a perfect Billy; James Coburn was superb as his exfriend and would-be executioner, Pat Garret; and Rita had a small part—one with no lines-—that was never destined to launch a promising new career for her. Kris managed to convince his old pal, Bob Dylan, to join them in the movie and to compose a brilliant score for it. But the film was poorly defined and was not a great critical success for anyone.

It took Rita Coolidge another five years and three solo albums to come up with the big one, *Anytime . . . Anywhere*. The success of that album came only after her previous LP, *It's Only Love,* which she was most proud of, failed to generate many sales.

"I think I peaked on frustration with that album," she says. "It came out and was the biggest secret of my life. I thought it deserved more."

It was mostly familiar Rita Coolidge material and style, with songs by Jackie DeShannon and Kris, among others. But what made it different and what Rita—and everyone else—felt ought to have been truly distinguished were two songs that were totally different from anything else she had ever done on an album before: "Mean to Me" and "Am I Blue," jazz/blues standards that were backed up by the jazz piano of Barbara Carroll (with whom Rita has made, but at this writing not yet released, an entire album of jazz songs).

The sound was truly high quality and compelling and as different to Rita as it was to her fans. Her voice seemed to naturally lend itself to the jazz style and tempo.

Rita says, "I just found myself opening my mouth and the sounds flowed out. It was easy, probably the easiest thing I've ever done in a studio. And the first time I've ever taken my tapes home and listened to them right away. I wasn't even tired . . . we might have gone on indefinitely."

For a variety of reasons—it was too big a departure from her usual style; the album's release got lost in a shuffle of other records; there was no single and therefore no AM airplay—*It's Only Love* was not the album that would break her out of her cult following. She needed something bigger, better, more commercial to put her right into the limelight.

Rita worked harder on *Anytime . . . Anywhere* than on any of her previous albums, and it showed. She had already cut seventeen tracks in preparation and was happy with them, when Jerry Moss, president of A&M Records, stepped in with a few suggestions of his own.

"He said that we could put out the album we had recorded and it would automatically sell my usual amount of records, about 150,000 copies," Rita explained. "But he wanted to try a more up thing and a different kind of sound." Better-known songs for one thing, some oldies but goodies, based on the idea that Rita's style and an already proven hit could only be a natural winner. The album was geared to AM radio, with the first single to be released just before the album itself.

Moss pointed out that since the adult rock market was growing so quickly and that more and more people were becoming familiar with artists like Boz Scaggs, it might be a good idea to include Scaggs's "You're All Alone" on the album. Rita's brother-in-law, Booker T., played her his arrangement of Jackie Wilson's "Higher and Higher" and it just "floored me." She went back into the studio and cut five more songs, "You're All Alone" and "Higher and Higher" among them.

"Higher and Higher" quickly became the Number One hit single on the air, and "You're All Alone" followed right behind it. If Moss's objective was to get the dj's to listen and the public to buy, he reached it in more style and numbers than anyone could have possibly imagined. The album itself went gold just a couple of short months after it was released.

Rita desperately wanted that first hit single, if for no other reason than to let her know she should go on making records. Once she got it, she was able to look back on her career with a whole new perspective.

"The person that did that first album *Rita Coolidge* is so far away," she says. "A combination of Bonnie Bramlett and a searching Rita Coolidge. Now I'm going for a little more class, like Natalie Cole. It really comes across if you don't care. If I ever did any image building, it's now."

The new, "classy" Rita is more visible on tour. Though she and Kris talked about her touring alone, they decided that unless Kris gets locked into a long-term movie contract, when there's an album that Rita needs to promote, they'd rather work together. So the Kristoffersons began their two-month, twenty-three-city U.S. tour with Rita excited and anxious about going out on the road with material from *Anytime . . . Anywhere*. It was a big move. For the first time Rita was as much, if not more, of the attraction as Kris.

"I've never minded being called Kris's wife," Rita

says, "because that's what I was. But I feel like I've accomplished something now. There were times in the past when I felt I was taking the audience away from him; I felt it was really his audience. It's more like I'm part of the show now."

The show. It's a combination of solo sets for each of them, then a sharing, romantic half-hour of duets, easily the best-received part of the entire package. One critic described them as "Another of those slobbering, mike-sharing couples," but Kris emphatically denies it. "We are *not* the Steve and Edyie of our generation." They are, simply, Rita and Kris and very obviously to those who see them perform together, natural, exciting, fantastic.

When they finished up their stint in the States and headed off for the European end of the tour, all the questions that had been raised months before had been answered with a resounding *yes.* Could Kris handle Rita's sudden success as a recording star? Could he deal with that success and his own need to re-prove himself to the public?

It was a screening of *A Star Is Born* that sent him cold turkey. It gave him just the jolt he needed, the kind of awareness of himself as a person and a performer that forced him to realize that his antics were hurting his career.

Kris had given up West Point, a Rhodes scholarship, and his ambition to be a great novelist to sweep floors and empty ashtrays at the CBS recording studios in Nashville. He hung around for five years, writing songs like "Me And Bobby McGee" and "Sunday Mornin'," making demos, and just waiting for someone to pay attention to him. His unusual background had prepared him for a lot of things but not for the furor that greeted the release of his first album, *Kristofferson,* in 1970. Johnny Cash had a hand in getting it made and released, but it was Kris's own amazing way with words and music that garnered the spectacular reviews.

He took his success west, to Los Angeles, and with a
ragtag group of musicians started touring every dive
known to mankind. Despite his rowdy, cut-up act, the
critics were overwhelmed, and his public success was
growing in leaps and bounds. His second album, *The
Silver-Tongued Devil and I,* was another smash. But
Border Lord, cut in 1972, was not, and his world started
tumbling down. The critics were merciless, and the
record sales reflected it. He still managed to give off that
Kristofferson charisma in live performances, but it was
getting to a point where no one knew whether he'd show
up or not or even remember the words to his own songs.
He was putting far more effort into having a good time.

He began his film career during this period. He made
Cisco Pike in 1972, a mediocre film, notable mainly for
his fascinating portrayal of a washed-up rock star— a
characterization he would later repeat. Then came *Pat
Garret And Billy The Kid, Blume In Love, Alice Doesn't
Live Here Anymore, The Sailor Who Fell From Grace
With The Sea,* and, of course, *A Star Is Born,* in which,
once again, he played a rock star on the skids. He was
making albums too—*Spooky Lady's Sideshow* and
Who's To Bless And Who's To Blame—but they weren't
making nearly the waves as his film appearances.

Other problems, plus the well-publicized accounts of
his feuding with Barbra Streisand during the filming of
A Star Is Born, made him take a real good look at
himself for the first time in years. He decided he'd better
shape up.

"I'm forty-one years old and I feel better than I did
when I was twenty," he says triumphantly now. "It's the
difference between going down a river in a kayak and
feeling in control and enjoying it, and going down a
river fighting for your life."

He did it all himself, his wife says. She was there for
him when he needed her—as he has always been for her.

But she didn't just sit home holding his hand and playing the martyr. She had a career of her own to look after, and his problems with reestablishing his credibility as a performer were something he really had to work out himself.

"As he grew musically," Rita explains, "people were not able to accept any kind of change. They wanted a whole album of 'Help Me Make It Through The Night.' Nobody was really listening to his records and what he was saying. They just wanted more of the same."

While Kris was fighting his battles, Rita's career was booming. She was as supportive as humanly possible, but it wasn't always easy for her. She had difficulty dealing with Kris's film career. He had been so very successful with it, it was becoming easier and easier for him to lose sight of his true purpose, making music.

It was depressing, but Rita managed to stay above it. She and Kris worked out the problems and she got right back on his bandwagon, defending his choices, and becoming the champion of his cause. When *A Star Is Born* was finally released, and the verdict was in on Kris's performance, she was the first to say, all publicity to the contrary, that Kris was definitely not playing himself in the movie.

"When I saw the film I was amazed," Rita enthuses. "I think it's the first film Kris has not been himself in. I believed everything he did, but it was not him.

"Kris is a self-made person as far as acting goes," Rita continues. "He's never studied acting; he just learns from other people. He's had directors who have helped him, and others who have offered him no help at all. I think Barbra was terrific with him in this film because she's such a driven woman."

What bothers Rita most, and disturbs Kris as well, is the fact that basically Kris is a songwriter, not an actor, and people tend to lose sight of that. The album he released about the same time as *A Star Is Born* opened,

Surreal Thing, sort of got lost in all the hoopla about the movie, and that hurt them both.

"Sometimes I see him getting bogged down in his films and I kind of see the light go out," Rita says. "I can see his doubt that he's ever going to get to do music again. It'd break his heart, just like it would mine, if he thought he'd never play music again. I think he could give up films quicker. Music is really his main love, but it's just been real easy for him to be a movie star."

Kris agrees, and films have been taking somewhat of a back seat to everything else. After *Semi-Tough* and *Convoy* and signing to do a film in England with Genevieve Bujould, *Hanover Street,* he's been concentrating more on his music and his family. He's just released a duet album with Rita and one of his own, *Easter Island,* and they're both doing nicely—partially because of the extensive touring the Kristoffersons are doing.

Rita's film career began and ended with her non-speaking role in *Pat Garret and Billy the Kid.* She's just not interested in movies, and in fact her commitment to singing is twice as strong as it ever has been. She was asked to audition for a part in Robert Stigwood's *Sgt. Pepper's Lonely Hearts Club Band,* but she turned down the offer because she would have had to compete with six other singers for the role.

"If they had really wanted me to be in the movie, that would have been terrific," she says a bit haughtily. "But I wasn't going to compete with anybody for it."

She and Casey do go with Kris on location wherever he's filming, but that's the extent of her involvement with the movie industry, and she likes it that way just fine.

"Besides," Rita explains,"I do have a little girl that needs one of us, and I really think it would affect her emotionally if we were both sitting in trailers and she was off with a nanny somewhere. She sure is more important to me than any aspirations of being a movie star."

Casey Coolidge Kristofferson is just about more important to Rita than anything else, even her newfound fame and fortune. If you got right down to it, and Rita was forced to make a choice between her family and her career, she wouldn't hesitate for a minute. Kris and Casey would win hands down.

Having Casey, Rita claims, was the greatest thing that ever happened to her. She thinks Casey looks like her, but has Kris's sense of humor and sense of "wacko." "She's insane too. It's absolutely wonderful," laughs the enthusiastic mama.

Rita compares the emotional experience of having her first smash record at this point in her career with having her first child when she was twenty-nine. She considers them both to have come late in her life, and both are that much more meaningful because of all the anticipation and waiting that preceded them. Her talent, and her personal stability, had the time to mature and grow significantly before she was handed the dual responsibilities of being a superstar and a mother.

Rita cooks, washes the dishes, does the laundry, walks the dogs, runs the Malibu beach house, and takes care of Casey and Kris with the same accomplished ease as any working mother. It means a lot to her, to be able to do that well, and still have the time and energy to devote to her singing.

"I have very strong feelings about family," Rita says. "I want another child. I have three now— two are from Kris's former marriage and I love them like they were my own. [They are Tracy, sixteen, and Kris, Jr., ten, from Kris's marriage to Fran Beer, which ended in 1967.] And I really would like to have one more, because that's what the whole thing is about. And if I have to back off from my career for three years, then I will, because it's the making of a person, and that's the most important thing."

Kris's two older children, who live with their mother most of the time, have always been proud of their dad; they have stood up for him ever since they were able to, no matter what he was doing—they just never could see anything wrong with Kris because he was their father and therefore perfect. It was having Casey, Rita thinks, that really brought home to Kris exactly how all his children were looking at him. It was a startling revelation.

She's quite a little heartbreaker, Casey is. She has both her mom and dad wound around her little finger—she's incredibly bright, can sing on pitch, and can dance up a storm. It was because Donny Osmond is her very favorite performer that Kris agreed to appear on the "Donny and Marie Show." Casey loved it and the duet Kris and Marie sang so romantically, and gleefully jumps into Kris's arms at every opportunity to tell him so. But then Kris and Rita try to do whatever they can to make Casey happy, even though she amusingly looks like "a tomato crying" when she hears her mom singing sad songs. She's a born performer, her parents agree, and looking after her is a career in itself. But one that neither one is willing to give up.

Kris feels absolutely at ease with Rita's new superstar status. There's no competition between them, and Kris is proud of his wife and that he was able to play some part in helping her career—although he had almost nothing to do with *Anytime . . . Anywhere.*

"I happen to feel a lot more secure than I thought I would about her having a hit," Kris admits. "I'm not going to get slapped with the accusation ten years from now that I held her career back. Usually success allows people to be better."

And Rita is not at all uncomfortable about the fact that her album is selling better than Kris's. She can handle the reversal in star billing as well as her husband can.

"The last six years have filled my brain with backstage and crowds," Rita tells people. "I haven't found a real good reason to go out on my own yet. Especially now. I think Kris's fans and mine might have objected to the pairing, but that's changed now. It's all very positive energy . . . I think I'm a good mirror image of him . . . and he looks as beautiful as I ever could."

Onstage they are as pretty as a picture. They hold hands, gaze lovingly into each other's eyes, and leave no doubt in anyone's mind that they are truly happy to be up there with each other. It's all a fantasy, they say.

"The chicks are out there looking at Kris and going 'Gaaaaaaaa . . . I'd like to be up front there with him.' Guys, I hope, are doing the same on my end. And then the fantasies become realities . . . and people just love it."

It's very natural what goes on between them. Rita is poised, having given up her jeans and Indian shirts—on stage, at least—for beautiful gowns, bright colors, and a style all her own. Kris is lean and muscular, with a boyish grin that is at the same time innocent and terribly cute. Without his beard, he looks even better than ever. Together, they are a fantastic sight to see and a perfectly matched set of sounds to hear. And although it might look to the audience as if they were putting their romance onstage for the world to see, in fact, it's just the opposite.

"That is [the stage] probably the most private place I've got," Kris feels, "because there's nobody allowed up there that doesn't work for me. Nobody can mess with you up there, and I'm getting to like that better than any other part of the day."

It's certainly true that the Kristoffersons are less both-ered on stage than they are even at home. Their house is surrounded by a high wall and several guard dogs, but even that doesn't always keep people from trying to get in to see them. Fans come from all over to try and get

Kris or Rita to listen to their songs or to just say hello, and they tend to ring the buzzer on the front gate at any time of the day or night. It's as if those poeple can't understand that privacy means everybody, except those special few whom Rita and Kris choose to see. When they're home, they like to lock the doors, turn off the phones, and store up their energy for the days on the road. They picnic with Casey, watch Monday Night Football, and live a relatively ordinary life. It suits them to a T.

They live together, love together, and work together. To be able to do that, with someone you love, someone you're married to, is for Rita, secure in knowing that her own career is together, "the greatest thrill of all."

"Before I met Kris," she explains, "my career was the most important thing in my life because it was the only thing I had to hold on to. I really wanted my life to be together—it is now. My child is more important than my career, but she would never make demands to stop my music. Casey's always ready to go on the road."

If Casey should ever make those kinds of demands, there's no doubt that Rita would give it all up in a minute. Life on the road is hard for a child, and on this last tour all three Kristofferson kids were along for the ride. It was a relatively easy one because they were able to travel on their own bus for most of it, with plenty of time to unwind and relax between appearances. But normally, running from airport to airport is a trial, even for the most travel-wise performers. For a kid, the excitement wears off pretty fast.

For the present, the cheers and applause are so appealing and rewarding, they even make the rigors of road touring seem like fun. It took a long time and a lot of one-night stands for Rita to come into her own as a performer, but she did it. It might have taken even longer without the support of the man she loved, but Kris stood behind her with unstinting devotion. He was there during all the difficult times and in all the hard places, as well as for all the triumphs and ovations. Their life is so reciprocal, it finds new expression every time they appear on stage together.

"I know I'm going to live to 112 because of the love in our family," Rita says proudly. "But I'd like to keep performing till I come out with little white braids and crutches singing, 'Help me make it through the night . . .' "

DISCOGRAPHY

Rita Coolidge

Rita Coolidge, A&M 4291
Nice Feelin', A&M 4325
This Lady's Not For Sale, A&M 4370
Fall Into Spring, A&M 3627
It's Only Love, A&M 4531
Anytime . . . Anywhere, A&M 4616

Rita Coolidge and
Kris Kristofferson

Full Moon, A&M 4403
Breakaway, Monument

3.
Olivia Newton-John

One critic has bitterly called her "as country as a kangaroo," yet Olivia Newton-John easily won the Top Female Vocalist Award from the Country Music Association in 1974. It made the boys from Nashville rise up in protest.

It's rather ironic that one of American country music's most popular singers comes from Australia by way of Britain. It didn't go unnoticed by the country regulars.

"We don't want somebody out of another field coming in here and taking away what we've worked so hard for," Johnny Paycheck said. And one of the more respected reviewers for a Nashville paper blazed that Olivia couldn't drawl "with a mouth full of biscuits."

The Country Music Awards are voted on by members of the association—broadcasters, agents, record company officials, promoters, and artists themselves. Their aim is not to honor long-term service to the field but to acknowledge the previous year's most popular people. Olivia was most certainly one of them.

The objection was that she basically lacked the roots to be a country artist. Unfortunately, country music no longer conjures up folksy pictures of back porch banjo pickin' by musicians with a long family tradition of country living. It's evolved into a style by now rather than a sociological statement.

Loretta Lynn, who also won an award that year, told the audience that she was glad someone new had come along. She herself had won four music awards in England and was not the least bit jealous of Olivia's success here.

Much of the grumbling about Olivia's win stemmed from the fact that although she was classified as a pop/country singer, she had never even set foot in a Nashville recording studio, much less the Grand Old Opry. Besides, technically a steel-guitar backup is what categorizes a song as "country," and that seemed to be missing in many of her records. The steel guitar, by the way, isn't truly a guitar. It's an electronic instrument with pedals and strings and puts that country twang into much of what you hear.

In any case, Olivia feels that country music is an arbitrary category at best. The fine line between country and pop has been crisscrossed so many times by so many people that only the record charts seem to pay any attention to those designations. Radio stations do not. Her getting the award did prompt some old-time Nashville stars to form the Association of Country Entertainers, a group dedicated to "preserving and recognizing the basic and traditional country singers." They would leave a lot of people out.

Olivia wasn't even at the Awards ceremony. She was in England, doing some television performances, and had pretaped an acceptance speech in case she did win. As a matter of fact, she didn't even know about the whole controversy until much later on. No one bothered to tell her that there was any commotion, and she never got her chance to speak up and defend herself.

"I feel like I was a scapegoat in the whole thing," she says now, "for some angry local artists who weren't winning any awards."

Although she'd prefer to forget about it, she does think her award opened doors and let a whole new pop audience into the country music world. Olivia wasn't even aware, at first, that music categories in the United

States were so cut-and-dried. When her music publishers told her they were releasing *Let Me Be There* in the States as country, she wasn't even quite sure what they were talking about.

"I've never claimed to be a country singer," she says defensively. "To call yourself that, you'd have to be born in that background. I simply love country music and its straightforwardness. And since the records have also sold well outside the country audience, it seems to me that we're broadening the acceptance for country music. I wasn't out to do anybody out of an award. I didn't put myself up for it."

In a way, it's understandable. When someone who isn't even an American comes and quietly steals away an award for something that is so typically American, it's natural that some people would get angry. But music doesn't truly belong to anyone; you don't have to be black to sing soul, and you don't have to be barefoot and blue-jeaned to sing country. Olivia doesn't even think you have to grow up with or understand country music to be able to sing it well.

"Music is in a constant state of expansion. It is progressing. One form comes from another. Country, pop, and rock are, right at this minute, being turned into another expression. . . .

"Music has to expand," she goes on. "You can't keep it in a bag. You've got to open it out, and I think it's happening."

It all seems to be a matter of forgiving and forgetting now. Olivia has since recorded a couple of albums in Nashville, and all those criticisms and gripes are like so much water under a bridge. And the gap between country and pop music is that much more closed. Olivia may have been the first pop singer to win a country award, but she certainly wasn't the only.

She is blonde, freckle-faced, and squeaky-clean. Her wholesomeness could be as American as apple pie if she hadn't been born in England, but she's slowly trading in her British accent for a country twang.

Olivia has that kind of fragile vulnerability that blondes often project. She also has those healthy, California good looks that outdoor living brings to the favored few—plus a city sophistication that is most evident when she's onstage. She is not a terribly complex person, nor, some say, a terribly talented one, but those are not necessarily the qualities that make an individual a star.

And star she is! She has won all the awards available to prove it, from Grammys to the Country Music Association honors, and her records have gone gold, platinum, and beyond! She's thrilled and excited by it all, but takes her success in stride and is not in the least bit conceited. She genuinely likes what she's doing and the way that she's doing it and wants everyone else to like it too.

Nothing in her life really prepared Olivia for this kind of overwhelming success.

She was born in Cambridge, England, where her Welsh father taught German at King's College. Her mother was German, and her grandfather was a Nobel Prize-winning physicist, Max Born. Olivia met him just once and says that being the granddaughter of Albert Einstein's best friend hasn't helped her much. "Look what happened to me! Two plus two is five!"

If Livvy—as her family and friends called her—was "mathematically useless" as she likes to say, her older brother did just what her family expected and became a brilliant doctor. She and her older sister moved in totally different directions, ignoring their studies and striking out in search of careers. When Olivia began to sing, her parents had already been somewhat conditioned by her sister's abrupt departure some years before to become an actress.

When Olivia was five, the Newton-Johns moved to

Melbourne, Australia, where her dad was appointed master at Ormond College. She lived there for eleven years and is still fiercely loyal to her adopted homeland.

There was always music in the house. Before choosing the academic life, Olivia's father had studied opera, hoping to sing professionally. He didn't feel he was good enough. Olivia thinks he was, though, and remembers that he once was offered a chance to study with the top bass baritones in Italy. He turned it down; he never wavered in his agonizing decision to be a professor and, as a result, his beautiful voice never saw the professional light of day. His Welsh background had always included music, however, and music was in Olivia's blood too.

There was always classical music playing in the house. Her father had a huge record collection, but among the Puccinis and the Beethovens were Tennessee Ernie Ford and other country stars. Australia really didn't have too much music of its own, so the American recording stars pretty much dominated the radio. Olivia's musical education was eclectic, to say the least.

Livvy's brother played the guitar, and she would sing the Top Ten along with him: "Lemon Tree" by Peter, Paul and Mary; Bob Dylan's "Blowin' In The Wind"; songs by Ray Charles, Nina Simone, Joan Baez, and Dionne Warwick.

Being a singer, though, wasn't always at the top of Olivia's list of professions. She thought she'd like to be a veterinarian, a natural choice for someone who loves animals as much as she does. But she wasn't much good at science and a bit lazy about school to boot, and she decided that instead of a vet she'd like to become a mounted policewoman, so that she could "ride horses all day and get paid for it." The only trouble with that idea was that Australia didn't have any mounted policewomen.

When Olivia was ten, her parents divorced. Her father was forced to move away, since the college didn't allow divorced personnel to stay on its staff. Her mother went to work to support the family. It was a pretty gutsy thing for a woman to do in Australia in 1959. Women just didn't work unless they had to, and Olivia found she was the only one among her friends whose parents had separated. It was a lonely thing for a ten-year-old girl, and one of the few songs Olivia has written and recorded, "Changes," has been about the effects of divorce on a child. She still gets uncomfortable, twingy feelings when she listens to the classical selections that were her father's favorites. They haven't seen very much of each other in the past several years, and the music makes her sad and depressed.

Sometime during her high school years, Olivia started to sing, "just for something to do." She teamed up with three girl friends, two of whom she swears were tone-deaf. Although her mother thought she was spending too much time on music and not enough on homework, her sister encouraged her, and her brother-in-law, who owned a coffee house, let her sing there on weekends. She entered a talent contest and to everyone's surprise won. The prize was a trip to England, which she didn't get around to taking until two years later. Meanwhile, she was appearing on a daytime TV show for housewives called "Lovely Livvy."

"I think I had the intelligence to get an arts degree in school but I didn't apply myself at all," she says. "Probably, I was rebelling against the whole academic thing. My sister and I both. She was the first black sheep.

"Then I went into singing at fifteen. By this time, my parents weren't shocked, just disappointed that I didn't get a degree in case it all fell through. But there are so many now with degrees who can't get jobs, that it's all turned out very lucky for me."

That Olivia ever got to London at all was her mother's doing. Olivia wasn't all that aggressive or ambitious, and doing her TV show—introducing people, doing sketches, and, of course, singing—was quite enough for her. But Mom pushed—she had that typically European outlook on life as education and felt that her daughter should travel and see things that would broaden her horizons. She even wanted Olivia to go to the Royal Academy of Dramatic Arts while she was in London.

So sixteen-year-old Olivia Newton-John arrived in London in 1965. It was lonely and difficult to suddenly be all on her own like that, and she wasn't at all happy. In fact, she was painfully homesick. Making friends was not an easy thing for her to do, and the London pace was so much faster and so more sophisticated that Olivia was totally intimidated.

Help arrived in the person of Pat Carroll, an old friend from Australia who hoped to make it as a singer in England. It was as natural for the two girls to sing together as it was for them to room together. They each became a little piece of home for one another. They were good enough to be able to get bookings in small clubs and Army bases all around England. They had begun to make a name for themselves and build up a small following. They were soon offered, and readily accepted, their own TV special. But before they could really establish themselves in the British music industry, the partnership broke up. Pat had to go back home.

But by this time Olivia had begun to enjoy herself in London and had absolutely no intentions of leaving. She was dating several different people and felt right at home in the club scene. What she needed was work, so she joined up with three young men to form a quartet called Toomorrow. They were given enough hype and publicity as the "new Monkees" to win them a movie deal, but apparently the old Monkees were quite enough for everyone, and the group dissolved.

Undaunted, Olivia just forged ahead. She cut her first single, Bob Dylan's "If Not For You," for Festival International Records in 1971. It became an instant hit in England and the rest of Europe, and she was well on her way to bigger and better things. She followed it up with an album, which also sold well, and with another single, "Banks Of The Ohio." That not only won her Britain's Silver Disc Award but also Australia's Gold Disc, and it was picked up by the Nashville disc jockeys.

Her really big break came from Cliff Richards, England's answer to Pat Boone. He took her on his European tour and to the Antibes Song Festival in France. She became a regular on his BBC-TV series, "It's Cliff Richards," and she appeared with him at the London Palladium, the Prince of Wales Theatre, the Tokyo Song Festival, and the Sydney Opera House.

Things were really starting to happen for the pretty little blonde from Australia. *The Record Mirror,* one of Britain's pop weeklies, voted her the Best British Girl Singer in 1971 and 1972. The Academy of Country Music gave her their Most Promising Female Vocalist honors in 1973, and she got a Grammy as the Best Country Vocal (Female) for "Let Me Be There" in that same year. She had never imagined that her success would be worldwide or that she would ever really get this far.

"If you were ambitious, it's as if you had to be aggressive and masculine and mean, and in Australia it was not a thing you'd own up to if you were a woman," Olivia says by way of explaining her amazement at her own startling success. She's always felt she had a sort of "hidden ambition," never quite conscious, but always there. If she had been totally without it, she never would have gotton to England.

"I think I just kept going—if you weren't a little ambitious you'd just give up. And actually ambition is a good thing. It gives you direction."

If by some quirk of fate Olivia hadn't made it as a singer, she'd probably be doing something connected with animals. They have no pretenses, she says; they are giving and they ask for nothing. "They're perfect."

As a child, she really didn't have pets, although she was forever bringing home the stray cats and dogs people tended to abandon all over the college grounds. Her mother was afraid of dogs, and it wasn't until she got out on her own that she could start having all the pets she wanted. Olivia vividly remembers one incident as a child when a garbage collector who used to drive a horse-drawn wagon was whipping his horse. Olivia, just seven years old at the time, got quite hysterical. She screamed at him and tore the whip out of his hands. It's a memory that has stayed with her, and one she hopes she will never forget. Being kind to animals is a philosophy she practices as well as preaches.

Olivia's ranch in Malibu, California, is a haven for all kinds of four-legged creatures. At the moment, there is one cat, Gypsy, a tortoiseshell; four dogs—Zargon, Domino, and Gretchen, all Great Danes, and Jackson, an Irish Setter; and six horses. Riding is one of her favorite forms of relaxation; it lets her forget everything for a few hours. Most often, she rides her favorite, Judge, a quarter horse, but Copy Jay, a Tennessee Walker, Eloise, an Appaloosa, and George, Alex, and Pipes all get their share of Olivia's time. She probably spends more on the upkeep of her animals than she does on anything else, and even her accountant told her that the care and feeding of her pets is her single biggest expense.

Recently, Olivia and fellow Australian Helen Reddy cancelled their concert tour of Japan as a protest against the Japanese tuna fishermen's slaughter of dolphins. The dolphins get caught in the tuna nets and are destroyed, and Olivia feels that she "wouldn't be comfortable appearing in a country where they have permitted the destruction of such beautiful and intelligent mammals." Helen backed her up, saying that the only way she felt she could protest this slaughter in a country that had been both a lucrative record and concert market was to cancel the tour.

Olivia also gets on the bandwagon against trained circus animals who are dressed up and ridiculed. Animals are "so sweet and straightforward" she says and shouldn't be treated meanly.

One of her pet projects is raising money for wildlife preservations, and she has also been in touch with Jacques Cousteau, the famed underwater naturalist, about becoming involved in his marine projects. There seems to be no stopping Olivia when she gets truly caught up in the causes of animal protection and environmental preservation.

Her involvement in these causes keeps her very, very busy. So busy, in fact, that she is not deeply affected by the lack of romance in her life at this moment. She had spent five years with Lee Kramer, a man she met in Britain shortly before she decided to give the States a try. Lee gave up a very successful shoe-importing business to manage Olivia's career, but since they broke up, he is only occasionally around to offer advice. Some insiders say they parted because of Olivia's very strong negative reaction to the idea of marriage. It frightens her. Especially since she went through such anguish when her parents—and later her sister and her husband—were divorced.

"I guess that's why I keep putting marriage off," Olivia admits. "I want to be the one to break the chain. As I get older, it's not quite as terrifying to me. Still, I know that everybody has to learn from his own mistakes, and I wonder what mine will be."

But she doesn't rule out marriage completely. True, at this moment, Olivia can support herself, so she doesn't need a husband to do that. And she's not quite ready to have children or even sure if she wants to have them at all. She doesn't feel she could be a good mother if she were constantly on the road making appearances, and she has no intention of giving that up. And she'd like to do some real traveling, to see and do a lot of things she hasn't done yet, and a family would tie her down. That's today, of course. Tomorrow might bring a complete turnabout. And Olivia has always said that she needs a man around to help her.

"It's very important to me, because you know that one person and trust that one person. I suppose, to a certain extent, they begin to live your life with you."

Olivia's life is dominated by her career, and it would be difficult for a man not to become involved with it. It was that way with Lee and might have been the same with the actor she was engaged to before she left London.

"You just can't get away from it," Olivia says. "If I got out for dinner, I'm constantly reminded of who I am by other people. For a guy to accept that is very difficult, and it takes a strong man to take second place.

"It's Mr. Newton-John a lot of the time. They have to have a good sense of themselves to take it. A lot of men are frightened by me, by what I represent, and my success. It's very difficult to have a relationship."

It could be a lonely life for a girl, but Olivia is far from lonely. She has her friends, her animals, and her career, which is about to take her in an entirely new direction.

People have always told her she ought to be in movies, and now she is. Olivia herself has always felt that movies were the next logical step in her own development. She had done everything else there was to do in terms of her career—records, concerts, nightclubs, TV—what else was left?

Olivia's always had her agent include a clause in all her contracts that would let her do a film as soon as the right script came her way. But the offers she had been getting weren't musicals, which she felt would be a perfect introduction for her into the medium, and they didn't feel right to her. They also had some violence in them that she objected to rather strongly. So she just went on singing until a script she felt right about presented itself.

Then along came *Grease*.

She excitedly tested for the part of Sandy, a fifties' teenager who sings, dances, and romances with John Travolta. She got the part. The producer of the film, Alan Carr, was every bit as excited as Olivia herself. "She couldn't have been more adorable on screen," he said enthusiastically. "She'll be a big movie star."

The role was perfect for her. She played a Sandra Dee type, full of bounce and cheerleader's charm, with lots of songs to sing—new ones, including her chart-topping duo with Travolta "You're The One That I Want," songs from the original Broadway production (which, by the way, has played more performances than *Oklahoma* and is just behind *Fiddler on the Roof)*, and some fifties' oldies. Besides Travolta, the cast included Dody Goodman, Eve Arden, Ed (Kookie) Burns, Sha Na Na, Joan Blondell, Sid Ceasar and Stockard Channing.

Olivia says making the movie reminded her of being back in school in the fifties, with a few extras. The script was changed a bit to accommodate Olivia's accent— Sandy is, coincidentally, an Australian. By the end of the film, Sandy has changed from a typical ponytailed teenager to a curly headed vamp in black capri pants and red high-heels. Olivia loved the transformation.

She knew she was taking a chance with *Grease*—whatever film she made her debut in would be a gamble—the more public she became, the more vulnerable she would be as well. But the film's a winner, and Olivia couldn't be happier.

As exciting as it was to make the movie, two things really got her down. First, there were the constant attempts by the press to invade her privacy. A weekly tabloid somehow managed to get what she thought was her unlisted telephone number and called at 3:00 a.m.

hoping to catch her off guard with some leading questions. They didn't, but Olivia was furious. The second annoying thing was the romance everyone was trying to cook up between her and John Travolta. She usually clams up on the subject, except to deny it. Such a love affair, had to happen, in the eyes of the gossip columnists, and, as a matter of fact, Olivia and John got along just great. But their relationship was no more than that. John's only comment about Olivia during the filming was about her acting. "You'll be surprised," he said cryptically, and that was that.

Olivia enjoyed the challenge of making *Grease,* just as she enjoyed the challenge of playing New York's Metropolitan Opera House. It was a scary thing for the girl who had claimed to have done everything but who had never "done" New York.

"I'm expecting to get knocked in New York," she said just before the concert. "An artist with my image is up for knocking from the so-called heavy critics. Basically, I know that I please other people, and you can't always please everybody all the time.

"I think the audience in New York will be blasé. They've seen everything—they can see everything—and you've really got to be good. It's a hard audience."

She tried to think of it as just another big theater, the kind she's played so many times before. But since one critic had dismissed an earlier performance by saying, "If white bread could sing, it would sound like Olivia," she was scared silly about how the supersophisticated New York critics might react.

The house was sold out, and the audience loved her.

She had tried desperately to climb out of that "nice" image by wearing a sensational dress for the concert, but it didn't much help. She still impressed the critics with her clean-cut, wholesome prettiness, and though the reviews were pleasant, the best she could get was that her performance and her manner were "pleasant, attractive, sincere, but not very invigorating."

She doesn't go out of her way to project that kind of image.

"I'm terrible underneath. Honestly, I do everything that most normal people do. I even have vices, but I'm not pointing them out. Why point out a pimple on your nose?" she asks.

At another moment, though, she admits to being slightly boring and, yes, nice. She doesn't take drugs or get into anything strange, and there's never been any scandal about her. She doesn't go around preaching about clean living or go particularly out of her way to lead the kind of life that gives her that image. It's all the way people see her.

"Right now," Olivia says. "I'm a novelty. Before I wasn't usually written about, but suddenly I'm an item. Luckily, the things I've seen so far haven't been nasty. I thought I'd get upset, but I haven't; I've just laughed. I find it amusing. All that attention is nice, in a way."

Actually, she just wishes people would pay more attention to her singing than to her pretty face and wholesome image. She wonders whether her talent would be more important if she were less attractive. But unless she drastically changes her selection of songs, the wholesome, romantic feelings her music elicits will always be there.

"The world is turning to romance in every area," she philosophizes. "There are more women in films and violence is slowly disappearing. The success of "Charlie's Angels" proves that people like to look at pretty things."

People also have a need for romantic, pretty songs, she believes, which might explain why "I Honestly Love You," a song she recorded in 1974, was reissued a second time. A survey among people who don't usually call their friendly local radio stations with requests showed that the song was the most "passively requested" one in the country. Nobody requested it, but everybody loved it when it was played on the air. A bit of media silliness, perhaps, but the lyrics actually have a great meaning for Olivia—which is the way she picks all her songs—and obviously to her listeners as well.

Olivia's one of the dwindling number of singers around who doesn't write very much of her own material. She's written a few things, "Changes" for one and "Don't Ask A Friend" from her album, *Making A Good Thing Better,* and she wants to write more. She has a box of poems and lyrics that she hasn't finished the music to, but she's planning to get around to it. Meanwhile, she gets most of her material from other artists' albums, and some comes in the mail—demo tapes from all kinds of people that Olivia and her producer, John Farrar, really do listen to and evaluate. In fact, two of her favorite tunes were found in the mailbox, "I Honestly Love You" and "Let It Shine."

Olivia doesn't think her music suffers because it so often comes from other people. She honestly believes that singer/songwriters often get away with performing, if not badly, less well than someone who's really just an interpreter.

She must be doing something right. Since "Let Me Be There" in 1973, she's sold more than 25 million records, has collected five gold singles, six gold and three platinum albums, and three of her albums have been Number One on both the country and pop charts. The music awards that her seven albums and sixteen singles have collected are truly mind-boggling. Everything from Grammys and Country Music Awards to *Cashbox, Billboard,* and *Record World* honors.

She'd rather be known as just a singer than as a country or pop singer because she likes all kind of music. And *Don't Stop Believin',* the first album cut in Nashville, was made there not because she was trying to establish herself in the country genre but because the right musicians were there, the ones with a feel for her kind of music.

"This thing about 'hard country' and 'soft country' music just doesn't make it for me—it's all music," Olivia says. "Country music has a style and I love it for its simplicity. But I also believe you can't put a passport on music. It doesn't belong to one section of the country.

"Music is international; the notes, the sounds, belong to anyone who can sing them."

That might explain why on *Making A Good Thing Better,* Olivia tried a song that would just possibly make people sit up and take notice. "Don't Cry For Me, Argentina," from the Broadway show *Evita,* is a lush, moving ballad that might easily put Olivia in the same league with other adult entertainers. She was anxious to do it and to release it as a single, because she felt it would be the very thing to end her "cute" image.

"When you don't know whether people like you for your singing or your looks, it really shatters your confidence," she moans. One reviewer indicated that she really couldn't sing but might make a great model or airline stewardess. It hurt. Even though Olivia is aware of the fact that she's pretty, she also knows she can sing. She's not great, mind you, but she is constantly improving, and that's the most important thing.

She's a strong lady with a lot of stamina; her relentless schedule proves it. The first eight months of 1977 were taken up with cutting her seventh album, touring to promote it, developing and trying out a new nightclub act, doing a couple of TV specials, and filming *Grease.* She toured thirty-three cities in forty days, flying cross-country in a rented 707 Starship that carried Olivia, seven musicians, her manager and wardrobe lady, and three lighting engineers. It was a big change from her first tours, when she traveled around in a bus.

She ended that hectic tour of one-nighters with a

week-long stint in Las Vegas, which, after jumping around so much, came as a big relief. Las Vegas really isn't her sort of thing. She doesn't gamble, and she's not much of a drinker; it was too hot to go outside, and there wasn't very much to do. But the audiences were good and appreciative, and somehow, once she gets on the stage, her adrenalin starts going and she's just fine.

Once the filming of *Grease* was over, she was able to go home to Malibu and relax. There were promotional tours and such for the film, and a TV special to rehearse for, but it was a nice, easy time for her.

She's most at home in Malibu, with the phone turned off and her feet bare, occasionally coming into town to go to a movie with a friend or to browse, relatively unrecognized, in record stores, checking on her own sales. She's found it difficult to make lots of friends here, probably because like most people in the limelight she's discovered that it's hard to really know just why people want to be friendly—for yourself or for your star status. She doesn't have so much time to spend with people she's not sure about, so Olivia tends to make rather quick decisions about prospective buddies. Helen Reddy is one, so is Dolly Parton, and Fleur Thiemeyer, a designer, another. She tries to keep her personal life private just because there's so little of it.

She's close with her mother and sister, although both are in England. She believes she and her mom have a telepathic communication and that either one always knows when the other is in trouble or having problems. Olivia even had a dream about her sister's about-to-be-born baby. She woke up at 5:00 a.m. one morning having dreamt that her sister's curly headed, black-haired baby boy had arrived on September 26. Since both her sister and brother-in-law were blonde, she didn't give it too much thought. But at 10:00 a.m., when she spoke to her brother-in-law, she found out that exactly five hours earlier, at the moment she had woken up, her sister had given birth to a bouncing baby boy—with curly black hair. It was incredible!

The word used most often to describe Olivia Newton-John, onstage and off, is nice, followed by pleasant and wholesome. Even when she sings about pain, as she does in "Please Mr. Please," a ditty about a woman who doesn't want to hear a particular song on a jukebox because it brings back too many sad memories, she doesn't seem particularly pained.

For the past few years, the most noticeable music trend has been toward what the music mavens call "middle of the road" sounds. It's romantic, bland, sentimental, but definitely hard to forget. Long after the record is over, the bouncy music stays in your mind, and if it has a rock beat, chances are it will be even harder to get out of your head.

Olivia fits right into this category. She's not particularly into message music, as, let's say Joan Baez or Linda Ronstadt is, and while her songs are personal, they're certainly not autobiographical, like Carly Simon's. Her songs are by Rick Nelson, John Denver, and her arrangements are tinkly. Her voice is sweet and reedy, maybe a bit thin, but it perfectly compliments her material. She admits that she can't really read music or play the guitar and sings mostly by ear. She doesn't have to know what key she's in as long as her band does, and as long as she's getting people into what's loosely known as country music because of the way she sings, she's happy.

Her interpretations of her songs are pretty straightforward, with just an occasional trill or tremor. It's all rather unemotional.

So what? Her songs are hummable, even memorable, and she manages to get them across with an innocence and charm that's not hard to take. She believes very strongly that she is what she is and that time will prove that she's capable of more interesting things and more depth. She laughingly says she's not trying to do anything that will change what people think of her.

"People find what they want to find in a performer, and I can't really object to what they found in me so far.

"My image will change when they see something more of me. Not something different, something more. Let's hope there's something more of me in there for people to find."

DISCOGRAPHY

Olivia Newton-John   *Let Me Be There*
If You Love Me, Let Me Know
Have You Never Been Mellow
Clearly Love
Come On Over
Don't Stop Believin'
Making A Good Thing Better
Grease

4.
Linda Ronstadt

"In the first grade," Linda Ronstadt says, "I always thought it didn't matter if I learned to add because I wouldn't have to when I was a singer. I kept at singing because I had no back door. . . . I had burned my bridges. I couldn't add."

Not that Linda ever really considered being anything but a singer. From the time she was two years old music was her passion, and twenty-nine years later all she has to worry about adding up are the profits from her 60 million dollars worth of record sales.

Onstage, she looks fragile and searching, a waiflike creature clutching at the microphone. Her hair tumbles into her face. Her feet, in their multicolored striped kneesocks, seemed rooted to the floor. And then, she opens up that pouty mouth and her gutsy, driving voice pours into her opening song and no one can touch her. She is up there singing her heart out, shifting gears from the hard, rocking soul sounds of "Tumbling Dice" into the torchy ballads and succulent laments that have become her trademarks. Her voice moves, in waves, from a whisper to a scream, and there isn't a person in that audience who doesn't feel every tremor, every dramatic innuendo that energizes each song.

It isn't any wonder then that she has been called the most successful singer in record history. She's easily the best-known woman in the rock world, the number one concert draw after the likes of Peter Frampton, Stevie Wonder, Elton John, and Paul McCartney. Other women have made records that have sold more, but she is the only one who has had five consecutive albums sell more than a million copies each. Rock may traditionally have been a man's world, but she is single-handedly responsible for the breakdown of that state of affairs.

There was never a doubt that Linda and music would always be one and the same thing. She came into this world wailing, on July 15, 1946, in Tucson. Her father, Gilbert, who owned a hardware store and was part German, part Mexican-American, soothed his baby daughter's cries with his guitar and his Mexican lullabies. Her mother, a socially prominent, sophisticated lady, whose family might have belonged to that venerable organization known as the Daughters of the American Revolution, took a more scientific approach to childrearing. By her second birthday, the *ranchera* music her father loved so much, the country-Mexican sound that still shows up in her interpretations today, was well entrenched in her mind.

And then she discovered rock 'n roll.

"I was pretty much a radio kid," Linda remembers. "I just loved rock 'n roll, and I wanted to be a singer. It was really hot in Tucson in the summer, and we had a cement floor, and I used to lie on the floor because it was cool, with my cheek to the radio ... I was about five when I started doing that."

It wasn't long before she knew every lick and lyric on every old Elvis Presley song. Joan Baez started to invade the airwaves, and Linda sang along with her records and convinced herself she sounded exactly like Baez. The Mexican folksingers were always being played, and Linda picked up their style as well.

Her first public appearance came when she was fourteen, and The Three Ronstadts, Linda and her brother and sister, cracked the local TV station. They sang backup for commercials, a little bluegrass, and a little folk music, but they didn't exactly take the world by storm.

Linda was going to a Catholic school in Tucson and hating every minute of it. The nuns thought she was too giggly, wore too much makeup, and talked too much about boys.

"The big goals with the girls I grew up with were going into a convent or getting married," Linda says. "I never wanted either one. I just wanted to go on the road."

It was partly her dislike of school and partly her desire to jump right into the music world that forced her hand. She never before, and never since, has had any other kind of job but a singing one, and she says, quite frankly, "If I couldn't sing for a living, I'd be stuck."

So, in 1964, Linda picked up and headed for Los Angeles. She hooked up with a fellow Arizonian, Bobby Kimmel, a guitar player, and Ken Edwards, a bassist, and they became The Stone Poneys. They were three musicians in search of a style, finally deciding that folk rock seemed to describe what they were doing best. They tried to combine "the roots with rock 'n roll," and they wound up being miserable and without direction.

The Stone Poneys managed to get booked into the small clubs around the Los Angeles area and finally made it to the Troubadour, largely on the strength of Linda's powerful vocals. It was there that a new group could be discovered and catapulted to stardom from the club's murky depths. And true to form, a Capitol Records scout signed the trio to a recording contract.

However, they just couldn't get their act together. They tried for three years and three albums and finally split—on the eve of the release of what was to be their only hit, "Different Drum," a song written for them by the pre-Monkees Monkee, Mike Nesbitt.

Linda looks back on that time now and realizes just how little she knew about anything, especially singing. She had let herself be drawn to California full of family praise and with no proven track record. When she hit

L.A., the realities were rough to take.

"I thought everyone who came to Los Angeles got a hit record automatically," Linda recalls. "It's a good thing I didn't know better or I'd never have come. I would have stayed in Tucson in terror and been a miserable housewife with four kids."

Instead, just three years after leaving home, she suddenly found herself a solo performer, without the security that being part of a group affords, and with a record contract to fill.

It was the kind of life she wanted, but it was not the road to instant stardom. She worked mostly with sessionmen in Los Angeles, Nashville, and Muscle Shoals and established a kind of cult following in and around the rock hangouts of L.A., but she was admittedly rather lazy and indifferent about her music. She more or less just stood by and watched as two of her backup players, Glenn Fry and Don Henley, went out on their own and made it big as members of the Eagles.

It wasn't as if Linda was doing nothing at all. She recorded two albums, *Hand Sown, Home Grown* and *Silk Purse,* both for Capitol, and had a moderate success with her first single, "Long, Long Time." But her career was just not moving along as quickly and as forcefully as it should have been.

It was pretty much her own doing. She was unsure of herself, unwilling to take chances, and unable to tell her musicians exactly what she wanted from them. She blamed it on circumstances.

"It's almost impossible for a girl singer to put a good band together," she explained at the time. "First, women are just not taken seriously. They have to shout to get people to listen. Women are just not encouraged to make a living doing this kind of thing. People relate to us so differently."

There was some truth to that, especially on the road, where rock performers are put in a make-it or break-it situation. Linda was usually the only woman on the tour route, and besides everything else, she had a rough time trying to steer clear of any romantic involvements with her musicians. She didn't always succeed. She had almost as much difficulty finding sidemen who could move smoothly from rock to country sounds without losing anything in the process. It was a problem.

But there were deeper problems than broken hearts and finding adequate musicians.

Linda had a hang-up about her looks that led to severe insecurities which, unfortunately, were reflected in her performances. Being on the road is rough all around but particularly so for a woman. Linda claims all women singers eat too much on tour because it's their only form of constant entertainment. Linda was no exception, and the extra pounds added considerably to her 5'2" frame. And when she's fat, or at least thinks she is, Linda doesn't perform well. Her skin has a tendency to break out when she's nervous, and when she's not performing well, she's nervous. She's been fighting a losing battle to find some balance between what she thinks she is and what other people think she is—and see her as.

"I get pimples and I get fat, and my nose is too thick," she complains. "You can never look as good in real life as you do on your album covers. It makes me testy sometimes, dealing with strangers and all their expectations."

Yet there's no doubt that Linda has a kind of beauty that makes people turn around. At her thinnest, about 107 pounds, she is as weedy as a street urchin, but at the same time undeniably bewitching. She has trouble dealing with it. She thought, when she first came to California, that if she were pretty, she could make it in the music business with ease. It didn't have much to do with anything, and, as Linda came to realize, the illusion of beauty, especially in Hollywood, is just that—an illusion. She really got down on it when she made *Silk Purse*. She had built up this reputation as a West Coast version of Dogpatch's Moonbeam McSwine, and for the album cover she decided to go down to the barnyard and sit with the pigs. She did, at a local slaughterhouse, in full makeup. It amused her to be able to make a pictoral statement about all that superstar glamour nonsense.

Her hang-up about her looks was one problem; her reliance on other people to run her musical and her personal life was a far more serious one. She had a marked propensity for getting her professional and romantic involvements all tangled up.

Her first two solo albums were produced and managed by men she was dating at the time, John David Souther and John Boylan. If she didn't know what she was doing, presumably they did, although the results didn't quite reflect this.

"I'm a mirror," she explains. "A real reflective person, and in a way it's horrible because I'm always at the mercy of my own surroundings.

"So I need a catalyst, always, and I need a good sounding board that I can trust. I hardly trust anybody, period, and I hardly trust anybody else's taste. You have to find somebody that you know knows how to handle you, knows how to reinforce you without indulging or greasing you."

Unfortunately, Linda learned that when business and romance are mixed together, it is usually the business end of it that suffers. Her boyfriends might have known just how to handle her personally, but they didn't do so well with her professionally.

She couldn't break out of that pattern until 1973, when she finally got tired of shifting around among producers and boyfriends. Her newest album, *Don't Cry Now,* which both Boylan and Souther were working on, was in big trouble. She went to Peter Asher, who produces James Taylor, for help. It turned out to be one of the smartest moves she ever made.

Asher is British and has a most unusual background and one unlike that of your typical record producer-hyper-hustler. He started off as a child actor with his sister Jane (who was Paul McCartney's girl friend for a while), made a couple of films (*Outpost in Malaya* with Claudette Colbert is, thanks to late-night TV, his best known), did some stage work, and gradually drifted into music. It became his only interest, and he polished up his guitar playing enough to become in 1962 the Peter half of a British duo, Peter and Gordon. They recorded a few tunes, "World Without Love" (written by Lennon and McCartney) and "Lady Godiva" being their biggest hits, and made some mild waves in the soft rock world until they broke up in 1967. Peter had become more interested in how a record was produced than in singing.

He was studying philosophy at London University when he produced his first records. Paul McCartney asked him to join the Beatles' Apple Records to scout talent, and the first artist he found was James Taylor. They both left Apple for L.A., and Peter worked exclusively with James, his sister, Kate, and Cat Stevens.

When Linda came to him for help with *Don't Cry Now,* he decided that she and James would be his only clients. He's one of the few producer/managers in the business who, by choice, doesn't have a huge stable of artists under his thumb.

He was just the right person for Linda to look to for help. Peter is, and was at the time, married, and his relationship with Linda was from the very beginning strictly business/friendship. No romance.

"Peter and his wife were the first people I ever met who took me seriously as a human being," Linda reports. "Peter was the first person willing to work with me as an equal, even though his abilities were far superior to mine. I didn't have to fight for my ideas.

"All of a sudden, making records became so much fun. I used to get so depressed when I was in the studio I would slither under the console and go to sleep with the monitors blaring, just to escape."

Peter wears two hats with Linda, as he does with James Taylor. As producer, he acts, according to Linda, as both editor and contributor. If she comes up with five ideas, Peter instinctively picks out the most workable one and files away the "developing ideas in their embryonic stage" for later use.

As manager, he smooths out all the rough edges, making sure that the basic components of selling a record—recording, rehearsing, touring, resting, doing promotion and publicity—are organized and well planned out so that his star isn't under constant pressure to produce something.

He's not just in the studio with her, he's out on the road as well, comforting, soothing, and acting as liaison between Linda and everyone else.

"Out on the road," Linda says, "if I'm having a bad time, he has to manage the political dynamics of the relationship between me and the band; the band and the crew; me and the crew; the tour manager and the band; the tour manager and the crew, and the truck drivers. It's staggering when I think about the actual amount of work he has to handle."

When she's performing, it's Peter who deals with all the fans, friends and members of the press who want to get to Linda. It's an area in which he particularly shines. Says Linda, "He's real good at dealing with those people, keeping them from moving in on me like a herd of barracudas until there's no flesh left on my bones."

It's all part of the Asher style, the protective appreciation and understanding of his clients. Because he only works with the two of them—a fact that both Linda and James appreciate greatly—he has the time to worry about everything, from the selection of songs to the buying of advertising time, with all the important little things in between—lighting, stage sets, tour structure, sound equipment—details he'd have to leave to a staff if he had more clients to worry about.

Peter helps Linda choose and arrange her songs, adds whatever's necessary in terms of technical backup, eases bruised egos—of which there are always many in a recording session—and is so enthusiastic about the whole process that he manages to make it absolutely contagious. And while he's all over the place and into everything, he never infringes upon territory where he's not wanted or not qualified.

"I never have the feeling that he's trying to flesh out his frail identity with anyone else's, and I think a lot of producers do," Linda says. "He doesn't play games or try to live vicariously or live out his fantasies of what he could be as an artist through his artists." He encourages and supports Linda, and she trusts his good taste and judgment—something she has, in the past, been reluctant to do. His values are ones that Linda can put her faith in, and if Peter tells her she's good, she's got to believe it.

"Linda is brilliant musically," Peter says proudly. "Her voice is qualitatively exceptional." He claims the noticeable improvement in her voice and her stage presence is mostly her own doing—he might tell her what he likes and doesn't like, but she's her own harshest critic. He's helped her loosen up and removed the kind of obstacles from her path that used to make her worry so much.

"Linda feels more in control of her career; she knows when she has a month off, when she has to do an album," Asher says. "She can see a pattern, a kind of reality to things. It's more like working for a living, as opposed to going through all the craziness. Before, she always felt that events were just rushing her along . . . in a direction that was really up to the wind."

Linda can't imagine ever working with another producer/manager. She and Peter have learned to tolerate each other's insecurities and make them work positively in every way. Sometimes, sure, they get angry at each other—that's all part of the game—but they work it out. Peter, above all, is fair and honest and right up front about what he means. Working with him, both Linda and James agree, is a very positive thing.

Just how positive a thing showed up rather pointedly in the reviews of the first Ronstadt album produced solely by Peter Asher, *Heart Like A Wheel*. With *Don't Cry Now,* which had had three producers, the critics allowed that Linda had finally found out how to be "emotional in her music, how to sing as if she really means it." The album emphasized her "skills in aching romantic ballads" and established her as a "terrific, straight-ahead rock 'n roll singer." Her way with country and western songs, the same critics said, made this album "a charmer."

Heart Like A Wheel brought forth even more glowing praise. It was an impressive piece of work, with two hit singles, "You're No Good" and "When Will I Be Loved." The lyrics of the title song, according to one newspaper, "distills the themes of the album and also underscores the essence of Ronstadt's vocal persona. No pop singer so completely embodies the mystical Western girl-woman, hurt yet strong, and entirely feminine in the traditional sense."

It was a "fragile, heartbroken album," another reviewer gushed, in which Linda managed to "create a recording of consistent excellence in all departments—material, production, and performance—but also, at last, to articulate that public self-image and make it work for her."

The listener could really get into Linda's problems through her choice and delivery of songs; she radiated power and energy and had, at last, learned to assert her voice, to start singing better and with the kind of confidence and authority to make her the known quantity she always should have been.

Linda took to the road to promote the album. But this time, it was a little different. She had Peter Asher to run interference for her and to make sure that everything was going smoothly all along the way. Linda is one of those performers who is even better in person than she is on recordings. She can be cute or sultry, down-home country or a "belter," but whatever pose she strikes, she is a true professional, in complete control of her audience and her band. It shows up best when she's on stage.

Most of the time.

Linda admittedly still has some difficulties with it all. She does get nervous—sometimes she giggles, sometimes she cries, occasionally she'll even throw up. Real success is kind of frightening, and real success arrived with a bang in the form of *Heart Like A Wheel*. When it hit the Number One spot on the charts, leaving Led Zeppelin and Elton John in its wake, Linda "walked around apologizing every day. I could see that my supposed friends resented me. I went around going 'I'm not that good of a singer . . .' And I got so self-conscious that when I went onstage, I couldn't sing at all. It almost made me go crazy. . . ."

She learned to deal with a lot of that anxiety with the help of a psychiatrist. Therapy made her feel stronger, more comfortable with what she says was the reality of what life was like. It helped make her stop feeling guilty about her success.

Although the *Heart Like A Wheel* tour in 1975 was easier than any of her previous ones, she still calls it the most miserable one in her life. She felt "unworthy," despite her new-found and well-deserved success. But she realized, finally, that she had indeed worked very hard to get it and that, in fact, she deserved it and should have no qualms about enjoying it. But it took some very anguished months to come to that realization. And it was the kind of anguish that would surface again as Linda's success and popularity grew even greater.

She's always had her fears about appearing in public, and this apprehension is always reflected in the way she performs onstage. While her voice is magnificent, she sometimes just plants herself in front of the microphone and sings, almost unemotionally, as if by rote. Or she'll hide behind one of her musicians, as if looking to him for protection from herself or from the people watching her. It's Linda. What you see is what you get, and there's no duplicity in her appearance.

"I'm never a different person offstage than I am onstage," she confesses. "I don't have a stage personality." Which is why, if she's going through some particularly difficult problems at the time, they show up in her performance.

"You feel incredibly self-conscious when you stand onstage, because everyone is looking at you, and they expect you to do something."

Linda's problems in that respect are the exact opposite of so many performers who make large crowds and screaming audiences their only forms of true expression. She'd much rather play small arenas and establish a one-to-one kind of relationship with her audiences, but she can't always get that feeling of closeness she likes. Sometimes her problems are personal; sometimes it's the pressure of working with a new band or just being on the tail end of a long tour. She always seems to have those nagging doubts about the quality of her success.

She used to believe that being a star would solve all her problems, and while it does usually mean that the best of everything—the top musicians, equipment, and staff—blend together to make a performance seem smooth and effortless, it doesn't always solve the per-

sonal stuff. To Linda, all the applause and even the gold
records don't reaffirm her success as much as knowing
she had a good night onstage. That's when she feels
surest that what she's doing is the right and best thing
for her. But then, there are those nights when she just
doesn't think she's been that great, and she gets doubly
nervous. Even if the audience likes her, it's not always
enough for this woman, whose struggle for perfection is
a never-ending one.

"It's just that peer recognition has always been the
most important thing for me," she says. "Since I always
liked music and hung around with musicians, I wanted
to be a real good singer.

"Having a hit record when I was twenty-one made me
feel real visible to the music community and I didn't feel
I was ready for that examination. I wasn't very good and
it made me feel embarrassed. I felt people in the business
resented me. I still struggle with that."

Ironically, it was one of music's most respected—and
probably most talked-about—rock superstars who first
gave Linda a clearer perspective on what she was doing.
Mick Jagger came to see her backstage one night and
told her to sing more rock and fewer ballads—it was
where her strength lay. (He did exactly the same thing
for Carly Simon, and it worked for her too.) Linda listened, and a Stones' tune, "Tumbling Dice," became
one of her most rousing, rowdiest concert numbers. It
made her feel good, too, to be able to sing it well, with
the kind of excitement that got people moving in their
seats. The first time she sang it in public, it was like
magic. She just got up there on the stage, and there was
no stopping her. She was aggressive and forceful, and
everyone felt it.

Linda admires Mick greatly, his strength and
brightness, and was happy to have him as her tour guide
when she was in London. But she's aware, too, that
Mick Jagger is "as bad as they say, and as good" and

that she had to avoid being sucked into his universe, if only to keep from being left hanging there alone when he decided he had had enough.

They have been linked romantically, Linda and Mick, but then again Linda has been linked with so many different personalities, it's hard to keep track. In one gossip column or another she's always off with some man or another, most of whom she hasn't even met. She's always liked to flirt, but she feels that it's all been overdone, and there's more to her than that. She's worried that people won't want to be seen with her because she's got this reputation as a "carousing rock 'n roller." And she's afraid that her fans will be disenchanted with her because of all the stuff about her personal life that gets printed.

That's why she's been so very careful about her relationship with California's governor, Jerry Brown.

Her success as a rock singer has certainly opened up new areas of involvement for her and broadened her circle of friends to include not just the biggies in the rock world but people like Watergate journalist Carl Bernstein, political activist Tom Hayden, and Chip Carter—which led to an appearance at the President's Inaugural Ball.

After her last tour, and before her next record, Linda took a six-month leave of absence from the limelight to "cruise around and look at all kinds of lives. I met astronauts, TV people, doctors, politicians. I discovered there was something more to life than the music business and different kinds of men than musicians. I used to think they were the only kinds of men I could get involved with. . . . Now I know they aren't exactly the most trustworthy lot."

The same could be said of politicians. But Linda doesn't seem to feel this way. Her involvement in politics, at this time, is centered around Jerry Brown, and their relationship seems to be more than just a matter of her appearing at his fund-raisers.

During the recent rainstorms that devastated Southern California's coastline, the National Guard arrived at Linda's Malibu house with sandbags to keep it from sliding into the Pacific. Their action was by order of the Governor, and the less-fortunate residents of the area were furious at her special treatment. Jerry's aides claimed he did it because he looks on Linda's beach house as a sanctuary—it's secluded, well guarded, and private—and he can relax there.

It might all have been ignored if Jerry Brown weren't a serious contender for the 1980 presidential race. Pollsters say he is one of Jimmy Carter's biggest threats. And because of the emphasis on marriage and family in American politics, the governor, who has never been married, could be looking for a bride to solidify his position. Could it be Linda? They have many things in common, their Catholic backgrounds, their familiarity with being in the limelight and traveling on the road, their positive attitudes toward strong, permanent relationships.

They met when he was still California Secretary of State, and they both hung out at a Mexican restaurant in L.A. She appeared with him in 1976 at a benefit concert to raise money for his presidential campaign, and their friendship has been growing steadily. Although they both avoid photographers when they're together, they have been seen at a Hollywood tribute to Neil Simon, at a Beverly Hills dinner for a visiting Chinese delegation, and in and around the rock emporiums of Los Angeles. They were in San Francisco together, and Jerry gave Linda a firsthand tour of his home town; they spent Christmas in Malibu, and he has been seen walking the beach near her house many times. Linda won't admit anything. She says there are a few different men in her life right now but no one serious. "It's a dating year, like it used to be in high school."

The Governor isn't talking either. He's concentrating on the future and whether that includes Linda remains to be seen.

Linda is quite happy with her life at the moment. She is beginning to find the security she once searched for in other people—particularly men—in herself, and she no longer needs to define her own being through another person. She used to think that getting married would be the culmination of all her dreams, but somehow she kept finding all sorts of excuses not to do it: her career was just starting to develop and she needed time and space; she wanted to travel and see the world; the right man just hadn't come along. Somewhere along the line, she came to the conclusion that she wasn't getting married because she really didn't want to. Now, she says, she is ready for what she calls "advanced emotions, the more profound feeling beyond the blush of romance—a strong committed relationship."

She's looking for the point beyond which she can trust enough to really fall in love. "Being with someone where there's room for mutual growth is probably nirvana," she says. "I don't think I'm incapable of that."

Linda's $325,000 white clapboard house is right in the heart of the exclusive California beach community so beloved by musicians and actors as much for its tough security as for its gorgeous views of the ocean. She has a dog named Jenny, a couple of sports cars, but not much else in the way of possessions. She's not much of a shopper, and her clothes, offstage and on, range from cut-down blue jeans to cub scout uniforms, with an occasional ruffled dress for variety.

The one other major possession she does proudly own is a tour bus with five stereo systems and rugs on the ceiling. It's not the extravagance it seems at first glance. Ridiculous tour schedules and airplane hopping have always depressed Linda, and by cutting down the tours to more manageable blocks of time and by sleeping on the bus between shows, she's much more able to use her road tours as learning experiences to help keep her music alive and to teach her that much more each time about trust and respect.

Linda used to do backbreaking tours even in the kinds of places she knew wouldn't let her be at her best, mainly for the money. Touring is an expensive and often money-losing proposition. Musicians' salaries are high, especially the good ones, and equipment must be expertly and constantly maintained to perfection. Hotel rooms and food add to the costs, and it's not unusual for a performer to do three tours in as many months and still lose money. It happened to Linda. She grossed over $100,000 in one of her first touring years and still wound up deeply in debt.

Studio recording is an expensive necessity for Linda, too, especially since she doesn't write her own music and therefore doesn't collect the author's royalties that often supplement a performer's income. She has written two songs, both from her *Hasten Down The Wind* album: "Try Me Again," which she feels is so personal that it's almost too embarrassing to sing in public, and "Lo Siento Mi Vida," which she wrote with her father and Kenny Edwards. But she says she is an interpreter, not a songwriter, and writing is a totally foreign process to her. Besides, she likes to add, there are enough bad songs around.

Ronstadt fans, however, were disappointed that she didn't offer more of her self on her next album, *Simple Dreams*. Instead, she turned to songs by rock and country music greats—Hank Williams, Jackson Browne, Bob Dylan, Willie Nelson, Warren Zevon, and Dolly Parton, who added her vocal help to "I Never Will Marry." She chooses most of what she sings; Peter Asher, of course, has some influence, as do friends and band members. But every one of her songs, no matter who writes them, mirrors her own experiences in life and love.

"I don't ever sing anything that isn't personal," Linda says. "I can only sing about my own emotions, and I always wear my emotions pretty close to the surface. I don't know how to live any other way."

She takes that one step further in her life and explains that she doesn't really ever do anything that's truly out of character; if something is not authentically Linda Ronstadt, it gives her a headache, so if you see her being klutzy on stage, it's because she is a bit of a klutz. It's not a put-on.

"All I've done in my music is acknowledge that I've been hurt," she confesses. "I've been crippled, but I'm still walking. Ever since I was six years old, I've been looking for the perfect boyfriend. But I wanted to be a singer since I was two, and when it came right down to it, I would never give up singing for any old boyfriend."

Take her album *Simple Dreams*. It is an admittedly autobiographical one, starting off with an old Buddy Holly tune, "It's So Easy." She feels that the songs on side 1 of that album are directly related to her own experiences.

"When you're a teenager or in your early twenties, romance is the whole thing," Linda explains. "I thought so anyway, and so did most of my friends. We sat around the Troubadour bar every night waiting to meet just the right guy.

"If you weren't in love, you pretended you were. Then, all the problems came . . . the fights, the break-ups. Love didn't turn out to be so easy after all. There were always scars."

That's exactly what "It's So Easy" says. Then comes Warren Zevon's "Carmelita," about how a person feels when she finally discovers she's on her own—a little down-and-out, older and wiser, but ready for romance again. "Simple Man, Simple Dreams," J.D. Souther's title song, is a little about the loss of innocence, a little about the uncertainties of how a relationship is going to turn out. "Sorrow Lives Here" is a touching song about searching for love behind a facade of coolness; "I Never Will Marry" is not just a statement of the future; it tells the world that it's not impossible that Linda will stay single, that it's difficult for her to fit people into her life at her convenience. Not being married allows her to meet all different kinds of people, from whom she learns a great deal. It's a dangerous situation for Linda sometimes, because all relationships are in some way wounding, and there comes a point when you don't ever trust anyone enough to make a heartfelt commitment.

As if to satirize her plight, she ends side 1 with another Warren Zevon song, "Poor Pitiful Me." It's a parody, a tongue-in-cheek look at the self-pitying, unrequited lover that Linda sings at a fever pitch and with intentional humor.

The flip side of the album is that very special blend of Ronstadt that makes her so unique. She originally wanted to do an album of real country and bluegrass stuff, with lots of duets and banjos. But she also loves rock 'n roll, and here she combines the best of both.

She rocks her way through "Tumbling Dice," the song she learned from Mick Jagger, and countries her way through "Blue Bayou," the first single released from the album. "Old Paint," the closing song, is a cowboy ballad, superbly done.

This album in its entirety worked so well because Linda combined her own instincts with Peter Asher's professional judgment and expertise and came out with a winner. It was one of the few times Linda truly took command: she handpicked her band—Mike Auldridge, Waddy Wachtle, Dan Dugmore, Kenny Edwards, Don Grolnick, and Rick Marotta—and was so sure of their stylistic compatibility that she let them have their freedom with the music. She chose the songs and the arrangements, and everybody worked smoothly and comfortably together.

"I think *Simple Dreams* is a great statement about California music," she says. And the critics agreed with her wholeheartedly. The *New York Times* thought it was the kind of album that would appeal even to non-Ronstadt listeners because of its "more basic arrangements, and a growing maturity and strength in her music and her persona." The *New York Post* said that *Simple Dreams* "casts its spell like the windows at Tiffany's with elegant elements carefully arranged to show off some bewitching gem ... Ronstadt's unmistakable soprano voice."

That voice, Linda feels, is the most revealing instrument. It tells everything, and there is no way to hide behind it. Linda's voice is beautiful as well as technically impeccable, and what it shows, according to one critic, is her "power and vulnerability." She thinks of it as just "shoving columns of air around"; audiences take it personally and emotionally. Her voice is funky and absorbing, gutsy and touching, raucous and seductive. She is sometimes least successful when she tries "soul" rock; it seems as if the harder the music, the less believable she is as its interpreter. *Time* magazine says she uses the "driving energy of rock and the melancholy of country music to transport herself and her audiences into a region of night town rarely explored by a mainstream singer in the past two decades."

Even with all the adulation and critical acclaim, Linda sometimes does admit that it's lonely at the top. And it can be rough, particularly on a woman. For all her independence and feminism, Linda is not the Women's Lib flag-bearer. She believes in her own independence and in doing whatever she wants but not in being one of the boys. That was the way it was ten years ago; for a woman to make it in the music world, she had to cede her femininity and be tough, to live under "the shadow of Tina Turner, feeling we had to do hot blues licks," as she puts it. But Linda predicted that it would change, and it has. She points to Stevie Nicks and Christine McVie of Fleetwood Mac and the Wilson Sisters of Heart and proudly says that they were able to become rockers without losing their femininity in the least.

Her friends, too, women like Maria Muldaur, Joni Mitchell, Karla Bonoff, Emmylou Harris, Bonnie Raitt, and, of course, Dolly Parton, encourage and support each other in this. She's just beginning to make friends, too, with women who are not professional singers. The common denominator is that they are all women, mostly single, who are enjoying the new freedom.

Yet, Linda Ronstadt is undeniably admired for her beauty. She doesn't really mind. She admits that it has contributed to her success, and since she doesn't use her looks as a weapon but rather as a spunky and enthusiastic way of getting her audience involved in her music, to Linda it's just another trick of the trade.

One of her fantasies is to form a group made up only of women and to record and tour with them. She's sung backup for her friends, and they have for her. Her good pal, Maria Muldaur, has sung harmony with her on stage—when Linda first started out, she and Maria were about the only women touring extensively and were almost considered freaks. They pulled each other through some rough times.

Linda, Dolly Parton, and Emmylou Harris have made part of that fantasy come true. In a big, hush-hush secret project, they tried to cut an album together.

They met at Dolly's Nashville home in January and decided that Brian Ahern, Emmylou's husband, would produce it and that Linda's record company, Asylum, would release it (the three all record on different labels). The songs and arrangements were kept secret and not leaked to the press, but several of them were Dolly's own compositions. The band was mostly made up of Emmylou Harris's Hot Band, supplemented by some of Nashville's finest sessionmen. The record was produced in California, and a few members of Linda's band contributed to the overdubbing. No one of them actually sang the lead vocals; instead, they shifted harmony and melody among themselves in all twelve songs.

The result was not what they expected. It just wasn't good enough, and the project has been shelved temporarily.

"We have wanted to do something together for a long, long time," Emmylou Harris said. "We like each other and the way we sound together." So far, there's been some talk of trying it again, but with three separate touring and recording schedules to consider, it may be a while before they really get going.

Some of Linda's current strength and resilience comes from working with and learning from Emmylou and Dolly. They are both what's known as crossover artists, straddling the thin line between country and pop music. They came to it from different directions, of course. Dolly from country to pop, Emmylou from folk/pop to country. The three of them together are an incredible combination.

If Linda looks to Dolly Parton as her mentor, she also takes from her the kind of philosophy that it takes to keep from caving in under the pressures of performing.

It's easy to hurt Linda's feelings, she admits that. But people who do don't often get a second chance.

"I am not a professional victim," she says emphatically. "And there are plenty of those in this business because they see vulnerability as something attractive.

"I try to walk that fine line between being strong and trying to avoid being callous . . . I keep the door open with the screen door slammed and a strong dog at the door. That's the policy of my heart."

It simply means that Linda hasn't shut herself off from either the pain or the joys of life; she's just being very careful. She has no use for women who allow themselves to be victimized. She's realistic enough to know that Prince Charming is not going to come charging in on his white horse to rescue her from herself; she has learned that she's got to do all her own rescuing. She blames this attitude partially on her disenchantment with the media, which, she says, portray women as using feminism as a weapon against men, who are drawn by it and at the same time frightened by it. She's her own lady, or tries to be, and all the old wounds have only reaffirmed what she feels now.

"The central core of my being is strong," she says, and that strength is what allows her self-assurance to surface more regularly these days.

Again, it is a learning process. That seems to be what life is all about for Ms. Ronstadt. With each new album, she touches new dimensions. On *Hasten Down The Wind,* which some rock critics think is her best yet, she tried a little gospel, a little folk, a little reggae. She still wants to get into what she calls "Third World music and Bulgarian ballads" before giving it all up to find "grace in my old age." Whether that means she'll do chanteuse-y nightclub material in her dotage is questionable. It's hard to imagine Linda ever giving up her country repertoire or her folk-rock-pop territory.

Linda Ronstadt has sold more than 17 million record albums with the last five, which include a *Greatest Hits* release.

Her music awards just keep piling up. She won a Grammy as Best Female Country Singer and a Rocky as Best Female Singer at the Rock Music Awards; she was designated Best Female Singer at the North American Rock Radio Awards. Not only did she sing at President Carter's Inauguration but the Los Angeles Dodgers invited her to sing the "Star-Spangled Banner" at the opening game of the 1977 World Series. This was not one of Linda's shining moments, but then Robert Goulet forgot the words at the Muhammad Ali-Sonny Liston fight, and José Feliciano's rock version at another World Series was not exactly greeted with overwhelming cheers. She's been on the cover of *Time, People,* and *US* magazines, not to mention *Rolling Stone.* Over the years, it's all been worth an estimated $60 million, which also makes her, besides one of the best and most popular, one of the wealthiest women singers in the world.

She has, with her perseverance, no matter how her confidence has faltered, opened doors for women singers that five years ago were impenetrable. More record companies are signing women artists than they ever did; she swears she predicted, five years ago, that "a girl would come along to open the door for the white female rock singers," and she's been the one. That she has constantly outsold and outsung all of the others is testimony to her own talent. She has even begun to feel confident and comfortable playing the guitar, an instrument that has been, in rock circles anyway, traditionally male.

She has found, too, that Malibu is no place to put down roots; it's transient, the very essence of the Eagles' "Hotel California." But although she knows it, she's not quite ready to give it all up yet.

Ronstadt has been compared to everyone from Joan Baez to Ella Fitzgerald and Billie Holiday. She once said that she even tried to sing like Ray Charles, but it was impossible. What is impossible, one critic said, "is trying to imagine Ms. Ronstadt wearing out her range, her talent, or her welcome." Her exboyfriend, J.D. Souther, whose songs so wonderfully capture Linda's own emotional ups and downs, agrees that "her creative capacities are endless. I doubt if she knows the depth of them herself."

Peter Asher, too, thinks Linda has new vistas to conquer. He thinks she'll get more into writing and just keep on getting better as time goes by. He has helped shape her into the superstar she is today and has been instrumental in making reviewers admit that her version of Smokey Robinson's "The Tracks Of My Tears" is even better than the original, that Patsy Cline's classic and "definitive" recording of "Crazy" is pale in comparison to Linda's, and that she has made "Stones' people listen to a torch singer."

All 5'2" of her is behind the effort to blend her looks, voice, and natural charm into one perfect package. She is at once honest and therefore vulnerable, but at the same time a tough, sassy cookie. It is all very real, and that's why people love her. There's none of that "you can't get into my life" attitude about Linda. She is a strong lady, and whatever has happened to her has been because she let it. But she hasn't packed up her emotional expressiveness by any means. Her pain will be your pain, if only because she sings it that way.

"I'm a real seventies' person," she says proudly. "Sixties' protest songs always seemed too general and hypocritical too. Maybe I'm a very narrow person, but the experiences that move me deeply are the experiences I have with other individuals, whether it's friendship or romance.

"It's always traumatic on some levels. It's always uplifting on some levels—those are the things I like to express in my music."

DISCOGRAPHY

The Stone Poneys	*The Stone Poneys*, Capitol T 2666
	Evergreen, Vol. I, Capitol
	Evergreen, Vol. II, Capitol T 2763
Linda Ronstadt	*Hand Sown, Home Grown*, Capitol
	Silk Purse, Capitol
	Don't Cry Now, Capitol
	Heart Like A Wheel, Asylum

Prisoner In Disguise, Asylum
Hasten Down The Wind, Asylum
Greatest Hits, Asylum
Simple Dreams, Asylum

Debby Boone's Grammy Award certainly lit up her life more than any other honor during her incredible rise to superstardom. And Mom and Dad were there to share the moment. *Frank Edwards, Fotos International*

Above: There's an incredible closeness and
understanding between Pat and Debby Boone today.
But their relationship was at times strained in earlier
years. *Tony Korody, Sygma*

Left: Can you guess which Boone sister is Debby in this
early family photo? She's the blonde, second from the
bottom, behind Laury, the youngest, and in front of Lindy
and Cheryl. *Globe Photos*

Only Kris Kristofferson's eldest child, daughter Tracey, was old enough to attend the premiere of *A Star Is Born* with Kris and Rita. Four-year-old Casey and Kris's son Kris, Jr., stayed home. *Frank Edwards, Fotos International*

Despite a few unfavorable reviews for her part in *Grease*, Olivia Newton-John is ready to go on to another film. She feels even more comfortable on a film set than she does on a concert stage. *Robin Platzer*

Olivia's sister Rona flew to Hollywood to be with her for the opening of *Grease*. They shared an evening in Tinseltown with *Grease* producer Alan Carr (right) and actor Jeff Conway. *Frank Edwards, Fotos International*

Charles Bush, Sygma

Above: Linda's manager-producer Peter Asher has remained a friend rather than a boyfriend. The separation between business and romance has worked spectacularly. *Globe Photos*

Left: Linda Ronstadt, like millions of other Americans, has taken up jogging. Here she barefoots it near her Malibu beach home. *Steve Shapiro, Sygma*

Fleetwood Mac was never better than when Stevie Nicks and company recorded *Rumours*, despite all the emotional turmoil each group member was going through. From left: Mick Fleetwood, Stevie, Christine McVie, John McVie, and Lindsey Buckingham.
Russell C. Turiak

Carly Simon's spring '78 tour was her first road trip in six years. *Robin Platzer*

Whether or not Carly's smash "You're So Vain" was about Mick Jagger, there's no denying the definite resemblance between the two. *Robert Fitzgerald, Globe Photos*

5.
Stevie Nicks

She is the very heart and soul of Fleetwood Mac, this powerhouse soprano in a witch-black cape and slouchy hat that barely lets her blond head peek through. She looks a little weird up there on the stage, traveling across it in a random pattern, but then they all do, in their assorted costumes and stances.

But when Stevie Nicks opens her mouth to sing, and that slightly nasal, slightly raspy voice wraps itself around a song, all is forgotten but the sound.

Fleetwood Mac combines the best of the British blues and the California pop music sounds, and it is largely because of the contribution of the effervescent and volatile Stevie Nicks.

But Fleetwood Mac *is* totally a group effort, and to understand how and why it's important to trace their history a little.

There has always been a Fleetwood Mac, at least as far back as 1967, when Peter Green, John McVie, and Mick Fleetwood—guitarist, bassist, and drummer respectively—formed their own group. They had all been part of John Mayall's Bluesbrakers, one of Britain's top blues bands, but they wanted to play basic electric blues with an even purer "black urban American" interpretation than Mayall did. They added Jeremy Spencer and Danny Kirwan, both on guitar, and then they were five. The concentration of talent was overwhelming, and they hit the British music scene—which was undergoing a blues resurgence—like the proverbial ton of bricks.

They were exciting, electric, and totally committed to the blues form.

In three years they made three albums and a number of singles, all of which did extremely well in England. Just as Peter Green's "Black Magic Woman" was released as a single, Green began experiencing some personal problems and left the group.

"It was an out-of-the-blue shock to everybody," Christine McVie explains. "Peter had been quite happy and was starting to write this incredible music like 'Green Manalishi.' It was like he was being lifted. He's wrung the blues dry and already played fifty times better than most of the black guitarists."

About a year later, Jeremy Spencer left too. He joined a religious/spiritual organization to which he still belongs. Fleetwood Mac had to re-form.

By this time, John McVie had married Christine Perfect, a blues singer herself with a fine musical reputation. She had been with a group called Chickenshack, who had frequently played on the same bill with Fleetwood Mac. When she and John were married, both bands were touring pretty heavily, at opposite ends of the world, and they hardly saw one another. Christine eventually left Chickenshack to try it as a single, but she was less than an overwhelming success. She eventually settled down to being John McVie's wife and an unofficial contributor to Fleetwood Mac's next album.

They were now four, and Bob Welch, a Californian living in Paris, joined the group. He was really responsible for the merging of the mainstream Los Angeles sound with Mac's British blues—a sound that Stevie Nicks and her then boyfriend, Lindsey Buckingham, would further cement in a year or two.

Danny Kirwan left the band in 1972. They were down to three again, but it wasn't as traumatic as it had been when Green and Spencer left. They could have and would have coped with it rather well, except that their then manager made a colossal mistake. Because of all the personnel changes, Mac's American tour was cut short, and the manager decided to put another "Fleetwood Mac" on the road to fulfill all the remaining concert dates. No one was fooled by the charade, but there was a lot of confusion and finally a court injunction to stop the manager from further using the group's name in any way.

The McVies, Mick Fleetwood, and Bob Welch moved to Los Angeles hoping for a new start. They cut a new album, *Heroes Are Hard To Find,* and started a long and serious tour to back it and to remind everyone that through it all Fleetwood Mac had survived. When Bob Welch left to start his own band in Paris, just after the tour was over, it was okay. What remained of Fleetwood Mac—Mick and the two McVies—would keep at it and eventually rebuild.

The group was too broke to hire a new manager, so at first McVie and Fleetwood split the chores. Eventually, Fleetwood took over the whole thing, hiring a lawyer to work out the legal details. Late in 1974, he met with an engineer who was trying to sell the facilities at his studio to Fleetwood for future recordings. As a demo of what he could produce, he played a tape by Stevie Nicks and Lindsey Buckingham.

Mick Fleetwood liked their sound. But it took two months and Bob Welch's departure before he called them. Stevie and Lindsey had recorded one album for Polydor, *Buckingham/Nicks,* and had a small cult following, but at the moment Mick's offer to join Fleetwood Mac came along, Stevie was waitressing in Beverly Hills, and Lindsey was working as a telephone salesman.

"John and Mick have always been open to having a lot of people in the band," Lindsey Buckingham says. "I would never be able to do that. I would think it was real important to keep an identity. . . .But that openness is what kept them going for so long."

Now, in what was its fourth incarnation in eight years, it looked as if Fleetwood Mac had finally found itself. Christine McVie remembers the group as it was in its early years.

"Fleetwood Mac had this one-of-a-kind charm. They were gregarious, charming, and cheeky on stage. Very cheeky. They'd have a good time. Peter Green just made the audience laugh. . . .They had this tremendous subtle power."

They had always been, at the very least, moderately successful, through all the personnel changes and identity crises. Their albums made it steadily, if not spectacularly, into the Top 20 before taking the same steady course down. Sales figures, nice to have when they were soaring, were never really frustrating. Fleetwood Mac, whomever it happened to be made up of at the moment, was a way of life.

"You go to the office every day and you don't think about it in the end, you just go," Mick Fleetwood says. "That's what we were doing. Being part of Fleetwood Mac, playing through the ups and downs."

It was all a very natural course of events, from the very beginning when the band was formed. Records were not made specifically to be hits; it was potluck. Great if they were; satisfying musically even if they weren't.

Enter Buckingham and Nicks.

Without ever even appearing on a stage together, the two newest Macs joined the others in the studio and recorded *Fleetwood Mac*—the album that was to finally break the top of the charts and stay there for months.

The album was intended as a double introduction: of the members of Fleetwood Mac to each other and of their new identity to their audience. It had an energy and enthusiasm that made its wide range of songs and material work even more harmoniously than ever before.

Christine McVie's five songs were her best ones ever; the three each from Stevie and Lindsey matched them perfectly. They all felt the album would do well.

"We knew right after we finished it that the album was going to be big," Christine says. "We knew we had something special. We just didn't know how big."

It wasn't until after the first concert, part of a blitz tour to promote the album and themselves, that they knew. Again, it was up to Christine, who is sort of the unofficial legend-keeper of the group, to put it into words.

"We could tell by the first concert we ever did that it was going to be good. The first show went down a complete storm; there was something about the combination of people on the stage that was very special."

There were three factors operating on that tour that did make it special. The first was the individuals themselves. They had all coalesced into one very fantastic, smoothly running musical machine. The three songwriters, Chris, Stevie, and Lindsey, each contributed his or her own specific style—Chris's love songs, bluesy and ballady; Stevie's slightly mystical, romantic tunes; and Lindsey's bouncy, California rock numbers. Their singing and harmony has occasionally reminded critics of The Mamas and The Papas, a comparison underscored by Lindsey's strong guitar playing, which is perfectly complemented in the rhythm department by John McVie's bass and Mick Fleetwood's drums. The music was alive and aware, tinged with the same blues sounds that so inspired the original group way back in the beginning.

Factor number two was the group effort, 99 percent of which is the music, Christine says. "The writer of a song offers it to the band, but the arrangement is filtered through all five of us. We have three songwriters and a variety of musical ideas that hasn't even begun to be explored. Five individuals, all with very strong ideas.

We haven't even tapped our resources yet. There are no limits to what we can do."

The final and perhaps the most important thing that so distinguished this Fleetwood Mac group from all the others was Stevie Nicks. It would be unfair to say that she was completely responsible for their current status as a supergroup, but she has certainly contributed her fair share to their success.

Before her arrival, the critics felt that Mac, as good as it was, was getting a little stale—onstage and in the studio. It was Stevie, a sort of combination hippie-cheerleader, weaving her enchantress spells over the audience, who added the missing spunk and sparkle. She is beautiful, funky, sultry, wild, the perfect counterbalance to Christine's mature, earthy confidence. And it worked so beautifully. *Fleetwood Mac* sold 3 million copies and produced three hit singles: "Over My Head," "Rhiannon" (Stevie's song about a good Welsh witch she had once read about), and "Say You Love Me." None of the group's previous records had even gone gold; this one went past platinum.

"I think," Stevie says, trying to explain the phenomenon, "that basically the audiences really like us as people. I think they have a good feeling toward us in a very human way."

Instant success was something that did not really affect Stevie Nicks, didn't make her any less human. She's been surrounded by success for all her twenty-nine years, in one form or another, and she can handle it like a pro. Much of that ability was learned at her father's knee. Jeff Nicks was an ambitious, successful man who was at one and the same time executive vice-president of Greyhound and president of Armour Meats. Only heart surgery forced him to slow down and retire.

Because of her dad's corporate mobility, Stevie and family moved around a lot, from Phoenix, where she was born, to Los Angeles, Texas, Utah, Mexico, and San Francisco. Wherever they were, she was always "the star in my family's eyes."

By the time she was sweet sixteen, Stevie had come to an amazing and enlightening conclusion. She could really reach people, affect them, make them listen to her through the songs she was writing. Songs were her way of communicating with others, and the realization of the power of her music came on her suddenly.

"It was May," she remembers, "and I sat down and played the song I had written. I don't even remember who I played it for, and it wasn't a very good song—it was about my long-lost love—and I remember it was very effective. I was really upset about something and I realized that I could communicate that pain through the song.

"That to me had always been the essence of what I do —to write words and music that would get to somebody and make them feel what I feel when I write them. I feel that people would feel that intimacy in live performance if it was something that I really felt.

"For me, songwriting has been the greatest gift."

What makes Stevie's songs so workable within the framework of Fleetwood Mac is partially that they are written in direct contrast to the way Christine McVie writes her songs. She writes fast and never a lot. And she doesn't struggle over them.

"I write what is required of me," Christine says. "For me, people like Joni Mitchell are making too much of a statement. I don't really write about myself, which puts me in a safe little cocoon. . . . I'm a pretty basic love-song writer."

Stevie took her songs to San José State College where she worked toward a degree in speech communications. Much to everyone's dismay, shortly before graduation she dropped out, opting to join a hard rock band called

Fritz. Her parents were not pleased, but they were more than willing to let Stevie try—as long as she took care of herself.

"They wanted me to do what I wanted to do," Stevie says. "They were just worried that I was going to get down to eighty pounds and be miserable."

Stevie's parents had cause to worry at first, although she soon proved to them that she would be just fine.

Fritz managed to stay together for nearly four years, largely because of Stevie. She was the only woman in the five-piece band, and they all thought she was in it for the attention. The fact that Stevie was the real drawing card made their attitude toward her even worse.

"They would kill themselves practicing for ten hours," she remembers, "and then people would call up and say 'We want to book that band with the little brownish-blondish-haired girl.' There were always weird things going on between us."

To the band, Stevie was just the "girl singer" and no one was allowed to look at her in any other way. That "hands off" directive even went so far as to include Lindsey Buckingham—at least until the group broke up. There was always something between Lindsey and Stevie, but it never crystallized while Fritz existed.

"Nobody in the band really wanted me as their girl friend because I was just too ambitious for them," Stevie laughs now. "But they didn't want anybody else to have me either. If anybody in the band started spending any time with me, the other three would literally pick that person apart. To the death."

It was rather a lonely time for Stevie, but not for long. Fritz played whatever small clubs they could, but finally the internal squabbles and the change in direction in the music world gave them the perfect excuse to break up. And the perfect excuse for Stevie and Lindsey to finally get together.

They began to spend a lot of time together working

out songs and harmonies, and, as Stevie remembers it, pretty soon they started spending all their time together. "It just happened."

The natural direction for two rock singers trying to make it in 1972 was Los Angeles, and Buckingham/Nicks were no exception.

Lindsey Buckingham had come to Fritz from Palo Alto. He was expected by his family to follow in his brother Gregg's footsteps and be "another jock in a family of swimming jocks"; to go on and win Olympic medals as Gregg had in 1968. Lindsey felt otherwise. He became involved with a rock band, so involved that he left his water polo team high and dry and his coach screaming in rage. And when Fritz left the safe harbors of plain old rock for a hard rock variety, Lindsey easily switched from guitar to bass.

"I was just a young kid who thought it was really neat that we were in a band," Lindsey says. Until he and Stevie joined forces.

Los Angeles was exciting, productive, filled with opportunity. Buckingham/Nicks were scouted and signed by Polydor Records and cut and released an album, called, appropriately enough, *Buckingham/Nicks*. It was filled with songs the critics thought were "catchy and appealing," and while Lindsey and Stevie weren't making any headlines, they were opening for star acts at the Troubadour, among other places. And they were developing a cult following.

Record sales were not impressive, however, and they only got as far as making a demo tape for their second album when Polydor dropped them. It was then that Stevie started waitressing and Lindsey took a job as a telephone salesman. It was a rough two years until that fortuitous day Mick Fleetwood heard their demo. Money was tight, needless to say. Stevie would get a little from her folks every once in a while, and if she had wanted to go back and finish school or live at home, they would have been more than happy to support her completely. But if she was going to stick it out in L.A., it would have to be on her own and on her own terms. On a visit home, early in 1974, Jeff Nicks tried to set his daughter on what he felt was a more constructive path.

"He saw me getting skinnier and skinnier, and I wasn't very happy," remembers Stevie. "He said, 'I think you better start setting some time limits here.' They saw, I really think, shades of my grandfather, A.J. He was a country and western singer and he drank way too much. He was unhappy trying to make it, and he wanted to make it very badly. He turned into a very embittered person and he died that way."

If Stevie's family worried that she might go the same route, she was even more determined not to. Back in L.A., she and Lindsey auditioned for any record company that would listen and for some that wouldn't. It was discouraging, to say the least, until Keith Olsen, the engineer on *Buckingham/Nicks,* played that demo tape for Mick Fleetwood. If Mick hadn't been looking around for a new recording studio, and if someone hadn't recommended the new facility just being set up in Van Nuys, and if Olsen hadn't been there to play the tape as an example of the recording technique, then Buckingham/Nicks might have faded off into the sunset, and Fleetwood Mac might have been close behind.

Fortunately, it didn't work out that way. But Stevie and Lindsey did have one engagement to complete before they could start making waves with Fleetwood Mac—a concert in Birmingham, Alabama. It was sold out, 6,000 strong, and Buckingham/Nicks went out in style.

Joining up with Fleetwood Mac was a golden opportunity. But when the reviews of their first album together, *Fleetwood Mac,* came in, Stevie wasn't all that sure she was really any good. The reviews, especially in *Rolling Stone,* were not all great. The album was pleasant, they said, but a bit anonymous, and Stevie took it all very personally.

"They said my singing was 'callow' and that really hurt my feelings," she says. "Time after time I would read: ' . . . the raucous voice of Stevie Nicks and the golden-throated voice of Christine McVie, who's the only saving grace of the band.'

"When it comes to competition, I won't compete for a man and I won't compete for a place on that stage either. If I'm not wanted, I'll get out."

She felt, she said, that even though *all* the members of Fleetwood Mac were ecstatic over the album, that maybe she had only been accepted because of Lindsey. It wasn't until the record went gold, and Christine's single, "Over My Head," which Stevie sang harmony on, hit the charts, that she began to feel better about it. When her own song, "Rhiannon," started breaking through, all her doubts miraculously vanished. She was feeling good. She *was* good.

There was just the right chemistry there, and *Fleetwood Mac* continued to rise up the record charts at an incredible pace, no matter what the reviews said. They were about to start recording their next album when everything started to go wrong.

Within a very short period of time, all five of the Macs were going through some of the heaviest personal disruptions imaginable. Christine and John McVie separated after seven years of marriage. Mick Fleetwood and his wife Jenny were divorced after six. Stevie and Lindsey ended their eight-year-old relationship.

That kind of collective emotional trauma might have shattered a less-together group of performers, but Fleetwood Mac not only survived it, they turned it into their greatest triumph ever. What was going on in their respective lives became tremendously interesting to their audiences; it couldn't have been better had it all been planned as a brilliant public relations stunt. *Rumours,* the album that, after eleven months in the studio, came out of it all was better than anyone could have expected.

"When we started *Rumours* in early 1976," Mick Fleetwood recalls, "We were all in an emotional ditch. Everybody knew everything about everybody. But I was piggy in the middle because I had less trauma than the others. [He was the only one whose mate was not part of the group.]

"Recording is like an expedition—you can learn fast who you can and can't stand. But, remarkably, there is no competition in our writing. All material is chosen by consensus, and everyone seems to take criticism without putting up walls."

Somehow, even though, as Christine said, they were all "pretty weirded out," they managed to get through it. Mostly because, as Mick pointed out, they were able to work as a team in spite of themselves. "We are a lot more adult and a lot more complicated than many younger bands because of it all," Stevie says, and Christine agrees, adding that "all that emotional stuff gave us ten years in one."

It also gave them *Rumours*. It was frankly autobiographical, and no one minded that the whole world knew it.

"On this album, all the songs that I wrote are definitely about the people in the band," Stevie says. "Chris's relationship, John's relationship, Mick's relationship, Lindsey's and mine. They're all here, and they're very honest and people will know exactly what I'm talking about . . . people will really enjoy listening to what happened since the last album."

Stevie's explanation for splitting up with Lindsey was a simple one: she couldn't be a real comfort to him when he needed her most. She likens it to working in an office with someone all day and then coming home together at night. If Lindsey was depressed because he couldn't get some guitar changes down right, Stevie was in a double bind. She wanted to sympathize with him, comfort him, make him feel better about it. But at the same time, she was getting angry because his not being able to get his work done was directly affecting her work too. She just couldn't be both personalities at the same time.

Lindsey looks back on it philosophically, feeling that all the heartaches had a truly profound effect on him.

"I feel like I learned a whole lot by taking on a large responsibility slightly unaided.

"Being in this band really messes up relationships with chicks. Since Stevie, I have found that to be true. I could meet someone that I really like, have maybe a few days together, and that's about it. The rest of the time, I'm too into Fleetwood Mac."

It was lonely and frightening for Lindsey, as well as for Stevie, being apart like that. But he felt it was, ultimately, "a cleansing thing," and he's become more himself again. He didn't mind his personal problems being revealed to the world through *Rumours* either. "Just because you're in the public eye doesn't mean you don't go through the same problems as everyone else," he laughs.

For Stevie, though, the breakup meant spending a lot of time with herself. She's never been much into the whole dating scene, nor is she the type of person who feels comfortable sitting in a singles bar by herself. It would be really easy for her to meet people simply because she's part of Fleetwood Mac. And that's exactly the reason she doesn't want to meet them. She has dated Don Henley of the Eagles, and Paul Fishkin, head of Bearsville Records, but she admits, "It's not easy to be involved with a lady singer who's always gone. Paul is sweet and wonderful and understands as well as anyone. I'm not interested in playing around, but I do get lonely on the road."

That kind of loneliness is a problem of women rock stars in particular. Linda Ronstadt has complained about it many times, as have Olivia Newton-John, Debby Boone, Ann and Nancy Wilson of Heart, and almost every woman who spends much of her time on the road. Stevie particularly remembers the Rock Music Awards Show, when Fleetwood Mac walked away with the top honors, Best Group and Best Album. Everyone was tremendously excited, and they all trooped over to a giant celebration bash after the show. But when Stevie and her brother Chris got into the limousine to go home, it hit her. She was lonely.

"I thought, 'Here I am, we just won these fantastic awards, we've just been on TV, everybody is singing our praises, and here I am driving home in my black limousine.' Terribly alone. Sort of knowing how it would feel like to be Marilyn Monroe or something. It was a very strange feeling, and I didn't like it at all . . . It scared me."

Loneliness, and the fear that goes along with it, are only part of the price Stevie has paid for superstardom. Another and far more serious consequence has been the strain on her voice. She has a not-uncommon ailment among untrained singers, nodes on the vocal cords. It's caused her to stay bedridden and virtually silent for weeks on end while her raw throat healed; it's been the reason Fleetwood Mac cancelled several concerts during their 1977 tour. Even as Mac was about to introduce the new material from *Rumours* with an exhaustive trek across the country, Stevie's hoarseness forced them to postpone the tour.

It's not gotten to the point where surgery is necessary, although that sometimes is the case, but Stevie is on a strict schedule: a maximum of three concerts a week; no cigarettes; only a glass of wine occasionally. She travels with a speech therapist who is in charge of helping her retrain her voice so she doesn't place any more strain on it—even by merely talking. The sound crew is particularly attuned to Stevie's problems and try to adjust their equipment to compensate for her occasional roughness. It's getting better, but the healing process is a long and tedious one.

The eleven months it took to put *Rumours* together were harrowing ones for the entire group. When they first began, in March 1976, they were recording in the Record Plant Studios in Sausalito. Besides all their personal hassles, some of the tapes themselves had been rendered almost useless by a faulty machine they nicknamed "Jaws." They thought they would have to start from scratch, a pretty depressing idea at the time, and no one particularly was in the mood to even think about it. But somewhere in the middle of Los Angeles's porno district they found a small dubbing studio that would meet their needs perfectly. They immediately cancelled a fall tour and went to work on *Rumours*. They were able to take all the romantic discord and channel it into one of the most intimate and harmonious albums ever produced.

Much of it can be credited to Mick Fleetwood. As the group's manager, he made sure that everyone knew exactly what was going on; there was no pretending things were going smoothly when they weren't. Their peace of mind depended on not having any outsiders poking their noses in their business.

"If someone from the outside had been handling the band, we probably would have broken up when there were problems," Mick says frankly. "This band is a highly tuned operation and wouldn't respond to some blunt instrument coming in. There is a trust among all of us that would make that a problem."

Even Warners, their record company, stayed pretty much out of the picture. They were anxious, of course, to be able to *hear* some results and were concerned that it was all taking so long and costing so much. But they learned to use the time to their advantage. As one Warners executive put it, "Between July and February, when it was finally released, we were constantly saying it would be out next month, and the press was constantly saying to expect it next month. It was almost like teasing."

And Fleetwood is the first to point out that the album took as long as it did not because of all the problems but because they were all so aware that something very big was happening. And they wanted to be as perfect as they could.

They were obviously doing something very right. When *Rumours* was released in February 1977, it hit the charts at Number Ten. Two weeks later, it was Number Four, and soon after, Number One. It stayed the Number One album on Billboard's Top 100 chart for an astounding—and record-breaking— twenty-nine weeks. More than 8 million copies later, no one really had an adequate explanation for it all, especially not for the success of the four singles, all of which hit the Top 10 almost instantly ("Don't Stop," "Go Your Own Way," "Dreams," and "You Make Loving Fun").

Mick Fleetwood felt way back in Sausalito that *Rumours* was going to be much bigger than *Fleetwood Mac,* as big as 8 or 9 million records worth. He never dreamed that that would be a conservative estimate. He knew that every single person in the group was getting something from the others and giving something back in return. If that kind of interaction hadn't been taking place, they couldn't have worked together at all.

John McVie didn't think there would be such a commotion about the album or such incredible sales. "It's just one of those things—the right album at the right time."

For Christine, *Rumours* was "a lot of rewards for a lot of hard work."

And Stevie feels it all happened because Fleetwood

Mac is more than just a rock 'n roll band.

"We may have had the worst day in the world," she explains. "But when we go up on stage, there isn't a more unified group. I'm awed by it. It's because we're all having such a wonderful time."

They need each other, and they couldn't perform if even one of them weren't there.

"We may make more mistakes than some bands, but there's a very loving thing up there, and it comes across," Stevie says.

Even the record company couldn't quite explain the way *Rumours* took off and just kept going. The togetherness of the group itself aside, Warners claims they didn't do anything terribly unusual to sell more copies of *Rumours,* just the normal print and TV ads, and lots of records in the stores. And since singles are what ultimately sell albums, the selection of the four from *Rumours* and their release was done with the record company's usual precise timing. The first, "Go Your Own Way," was out in December. By the time the album appeared in February, it had already hit the Top 10.

Rumours is the largest-selling Warners album in their history, and, for once, recording executives and critics have found themselves on the same side of the fence. Since Warners wasn't doing anything special to promote *Rumours* any differently from any other Fleetwood Mac album, everyone agreed the incredible sales figures had to be due to the music and the people making it.

As one Warners executive described it, each one of the individuals in Fleetwood Mac is a "national archetype" unto him or herself.

"The incredible British intelligence of Mick Fleetwood—he was educated at the Rudolf Steiner School. And McVie is the perfect foil—he's greatly amused by black humor. Christine is just the essence of a certain type of North to Midlands Britisher. And then we have the flower children, Stevie and Lindsey, very practical, but also aware that they are love symbols."

The critics, from *Rolling Stone,* which claimed *Rumours* established Fleetwood Mac as a substantial musical force rather than as merely a fluke, to *Esquire,* which proclaimed the music on *Rumours* to be "exceptionally fine," were generally and genuinely impressed.

Put it all together—the band, the music, the album, and the voices of Warners and the critics—and any way you slice it, you still come up with a musical phenomenon. Whatever the real reason for the unparalleled success of *Rumours,* one thing is certain—it happened. And it proved Fleetwood Mac was more than just a "flash in the pan."

Fleetwood Mac followed the release of *Rumours* with an incredibly ambitious and extensive tour, almost a year long. All the while, they were thinking about their next album, maybe a double studio effort, maybe a live album. There were already reams of material ready to go. Stevie writes all the time because, as she says, "I just love to write. I would like to write for other artists, too, because I write too much just for Fleetwood Mac. The busier I am the better I like it."

All thoughts of the new album, as well as of Stevie's newest passion, studying ballet, were shelved, though, when Michael Shapiro, Fleetwood Mac's legal advisor, came up with an incredible idea: a series of three concerts in Moscow. Mick and John McVie gave their enthusiastic approval, and the Russian Embassy and the State Department were totally in accord. A Soviet official was shown a videotape of Fleetwood Mac's Santa Barbara concert and it was love at first sight—the only reservations he had were about John's cut-off jeans. Were they proper and/or artistic stage attire? The official was particularly taken with Stevie; if she were part of the package, it could only be a good idea.

Shapiro, along with a Warners executive and Fleetwood Mac's tour manager, went to Moscow and came home with a contract for three July 1978 concerts in Moscow's Rossia Concert Hall. At first they thought they would broadcast the concert around the world via satellite but settled for a TV special—with all the proceeds being donated to UNESCO.

"Everything, of course, depends on world peace," Michael Shapiro said in the early spring of 1978. "But I'd be shocked if this didn't happen. The time is right for a group to do this. Fleetwood Mac, being English and American, two women and three men, is internationally revered. They have taken a lot out, and now they want to put some back. That's what it all comes down to."

The prospect of going to Russia was so exciting that the group decided to take full advantage of the few weeks between the end of the hectic '77-'78 tour, which wound up in Japan and Australia, and their departure for the USSR by totally relaxing.

John McVie, who recently remarried, went home with his new bride to Hawaii. Christine stayed incommunicado, probably with her new boyfriend, Curry Grant, the group's lighting director. Mick Fleetwood, whose divorce from his wife, Jenny, just didn't work out, remarried her four months after they separated, and they and their two daughters, Lucy and Jenny, renovated their Topanga Canyon house.

Stevie, whom Mick once described as "intense, brittle, vulnerable" and taking her life and herself too seriously, was giving her throat a much-needed rest. She bought a home in the Hollywood Hills, which she often shares with her brother, Chris, and a couple of friends. She plays "housemother" to the boys, and they constantly remind her that she's not a queen and that they don't expect her to act like one. It's a nice, earthy kind of relationship that Stevie is particularly glad to have. "Rock is flash," she says. "The rest of my life I want to be normal."

That normality, for Stevie Nicks, includes all the

things a woman might hope for, marriage, children—at least two, and by the time she's thirty-four—and a home. It's all part of her master plan.

"I hope that I'll be living somewhere up in the mountains with a very pretty house and a piano and a tape recorder, just writing and going to New York every once in a while to shop. I love that too. But I mostly just like to be in a really warm place with a bunch of animals, dogs and cats."

It's a long way from Rhiannon, the good-witch trip Stevie slips into onstage, and it's a long way from Moscow. But there's no doubt that if that's what Stevie's aiming for, that's most assuredly where she will be. Eventually. Right now, she's having too much fun and too many good times being a pivotal part of Fleetwood Mac.

DISCOGRAPHY

Stevie Nicks and Lindsey Buckingham	*Buckingham/Nicks*, Polydor
Fleetwood Mac	*Fleetwood Mac In Chicago*, Epic
	Fleetwood Mac, Blues Horizons Records
	Then Play On, Warners
	Kiln House, Warners
	Future Games, Warners
	Bare Trees, Warners
	Penguin, Warners
	Mystery To Me, Warners
	Heroes Are Hard To Find, Warners
	Fleetwood Mac, Warners
	Rumours, Warners
	The Original Fleetwood Mac, Sire SR6045

6.
Carly Simon

Put Carly Simon into a small club, with maybe a hundred or two hundred people, and she's immediately and comfortably at home. But put her on the stage of a large auditorium or concert hall, and she's just as likely to get cold feet.

It's always been that way. She's almost painfully shy and even after all these years still gets cases of extreme stage fright. She loves to sing, loves to perform, but audiences, people, scare her.

Between 1972 and 1975, Carly made only occasional appearances, singing duets with her husband, James Taylor, during his shows. Since then, she's limited her own dates, when at all, to the kinds of intimate cabarets she likes best. She recently went out on her first legitimate tour since "Anticipation" was released in 1972. Despite this, she sells more records than many performers who spend 90 percent of their time on the road.

You would expect to find Carly a meek, reluctant performer. Instead, she strides on stage, oozing confidence, tall and toothy—almost aggressive. She has a very special way of singing, electric, yet elegant, funky, but perceptive and from the heart. She's not a folksinger, yet she has that folksy rapport with an audience that makes them feel every pain, every anguished moment in her lyrics. Her voice can be soft and silky or growl subtly when it sings its story. She draws you right in there with her directness, bares her soul, and expects you to understand.

"When I get up there," she says with a smile, "I seem to radiate, but I'm really radiating panic." You'd never know it to look or listen.

The shyness, the fear of crowds, the need to perform, started long ago for Carly; they're not merely the pitfalls of her fame.

Carly is the third daughter of Richard and Andrea Simon and grew up surrounded by music, money, and the easy life. Her father, who cofounded the publishing house of Simon & Schuster, was a frustrated concert pianist who never passed up the chance to sit down and play. Uncle Henry Simon was senior music editor at Simon & Schuster and a respected music critic. Uncle Alfred wrote *Songs of the American Theatre* and *The Gershwins* and was a founding member of the Goodspeed Opera House. Another uncle, George, was a jazz expert and the editor of *Metronome* magazine. The first music critic at *The New Yorker* was Robert Simon, a cousin. Andrea Simon studied voice for years and yearned to be a professional singer as a young girl. There was no lack of musical influences in Carly's life.

Carly spent the first seven years of her life in Greenwich Village; then the family moved up to a rather large estate in Riverdale, New York. Being the youngest daughter (the only brother, Peter, is also the youngest child in the family) gave Carly some very real problems when she was a child. She remembers having to fight for her identity, for a place in the family that her sisters, Joanna and Lucy, had already established.

"I remember when a new nurse for Peter came to the house, Joey greeted her in this very regal, sophisticated way. Then my sister Lucy said hello in her angelic way. And I thought, 'What's left for me?'

"Just to be *something*, I jumped up on the coffee table and did an imitation of Al Jolson. From then on, I was sort of the family clown. It was the only way I could think to get any attention."

She was so aware of sophisticated Joanna and sweet Lucy that Carly truly felt she had no sense of herself, no part to play in the grand scheme of things. The only time she felt really comfortable was when the three sisters used to sing together. The competition among them, while not always visibly fierce, was certainly enough to make young Carly do everything in her power to be better than they were.

The opportunity to sing together, though, came often at the Simons' palatial home in Stamford, Connecticut, and at their house in Riverdale, as well as during their summers in Martha's Vineyard.

"We used to have a little theater in the barn," remembers Carly, "and my father's friends would come up and watch us perform. All kinds of heavy people we didn't know were heavy at the time, like Oscar Hammerstein and Richard Rodgers, used to watch us do our song-and-dance numbers."

The Simon parents used to join right in with their offspring. Mrs. Simon had a beautiful voice, and both of them played the piano. If Grandfather Simon hadn't insisted that his son go into business, Richard might have been a professional musician.

But business it was, and quite often the guests at the Simon house were from that world. Albert Einstein was a visitor, and Carly was so young, she just thought he was a nice old man. Don Budge used to give the girls tennis lessons; his stature as a professional tennis champ was something none of them was aware of.

In fact, Carly didn't even know that her family was, if not famous, at least very well known and highly respected. It was while she was in the fourth grade that a friend showed her a Simon & Schuster book in the school library and said, "That's you."

She knew she was privileged.

"We had the biggest house of anyone in my class," Carly recalls. "The freezer was full of ice cream. I had a shiny tricycle. But both my parents were conscious of not spoiling us. We certainly had enough money, but we didn't have particularly fancy clothes. And we always cooked and did dishes."

Carly still does both. She learned it all at her mother's knee, and although the family always had a cook, it was Mrs. Simon who did the real cooking, with her daughters as willing apprentices. She believed that women needed training in all the domestic sciences, and she set about giving her daughters their lessons early in life.

As loving and caring as family life was, it wasn't without conflict. There was that old, nagging sibling rivalry. And because of it Carly developed a stammer when she was twelve. It was, in retrospect, a sort of lucky affliction—it made her sing!

Carly was shy and outgoing at the same time, the exuberance being her way of hiding the shyness. She was, in truth, even shy about being shy, and the stammer was so pronounced, there were times she could barely talk. Carly developed all sorts of tricks to overcome the problem: for words beginning with consonants, she substituted words beginning with vowels, and vice versa; for words she absolutely could not say, she found alternatives. It helped her talk and also strengthened her vocabulary immensely.

"If I were given something in school to read out loud, I would beg the teacher not to call on me. It was so humiliating. I would stand up and stare at the book . . . I couldn't get any words out at all, just 'eh . . . eh . . . eh . . .'

"One of my teachers, this terrific French teacher, said, 'Carly, you have such a wonderful voice, why don't you sing your answer.' And I did, I sang it in French. It was great. It made all the kids laugh, but they were with me. It was fun."

So singing became a way for Carly to say what she wanted to say, at school and at home. Her mother encouraged and supported her completely; the trick was a worthwhile one if it worked. What really helped Carly get the stammer under control and eventually disappear, however, was a boyfriend. She felt that people wouldn't like her because of her handicap, which, of course, only made it worse. But when she was sixteen, her high school beau told her he thought the stammer was rather charming. Well! Once she could think of it as an asset rather than something to pretend wasn't there, it became so much easier for her to relax and just let it go.

Although music was always a big part of Carly's life —at home either the piano or the record player was always being played—she never had much formal training. She took piano lessons for a year, but when family friends like George Gershwin or Vladimir Horowitz would come over and sit down and play, Carly sort of gave it up.

After two years of studying Russian and comparative literature at Sarah Lawrence College, she gave that up too.

"I thought of myself as being an intellectual," says Carly. "I never really was, but I liked that self-image for a while and tried to cultivate it. Then, Lucy and I started singing together and I thought that was lots more fun than going to school. So I dropped out, I thought for just a year.

"It was such a relief not to have to turn in papers and everything, I never went back at all."

The year was 1964, and the Simon Sisters began to appear around the New York area at folk clubs like the Bitter End and the Gaslight and on campuses in the vicinity. Carly had a terrible fear of planes, which sort of limited the sisters' engagements to local gigs. They had a small success, with two albums and a hit single. "Winkin, Blinkin' and Nod," written by Lucy. But Lucy quit to marry a doctor and have children, and for Carly it was the beginning of a down time. She just couldn't get her act together.

She went to London and lived there for about four

months. That, as it turned out, was not the best choice. She fell in love with a man she met there and came home to New York to collect her belongings for the move back. When she got to London, waiting for her was a letter from her man, telling her it was all over. So she went to France, the romantic Mediterranean, and met another man. But that didn't work out either. He wanted her to stay in the kitchen and forget about singing or writing. It was so tense, she used to wake up in the middle of the night shaking severly.

She spent four years exploring her problems. Ironically, a few years later, she was in a French restaurant and ordered the same wine she used to drink every day while she was living in the south of France. That night she began getting the shakes again. As it turned out, Carly was actually allergic to the wine.

During this time, Carly was living with her sister Joanna, who was beginning to establish her career as an opera singer. They shared an East 55th Street apartment, and Carly was pretty dependent on Joey for food and comfort. The old jealousies were forgotten; Carly was truly pleased with Joey's growing stature in the music world, and their relationship was closer than it had ever been.

Carly was doing a little writing, but not much else. When Albert Grossman, a well-known, and maybe a little eccentric, rock manager told her that he would make her a female Dylan, it looked like the golden opportunity. The only trouble was, Carly couldn't sing like Dylan, and the entire effort was a dismal failure.

She cut a single for Grossman, "Baby Let Me Follow You Down," in 1966. Dylan himself got involved; he rewrote the lyrics to fit Carly's style. At a Woodstock recording session, with the full weight of some of Rock's real heavies—The Band, Robbie Robertson, Al Kooper, Mike Bloomfield, and Richie Havens singing background vocals—it was done, fast, sloppy, and never to be released. They had tried to mold Carly into something she clearly wasn't, and she went along with it because she wanted to be loved.

Naturally, Carly was disappointed. She felt diminished, used, that they didn't like her singing. The fact that no one had even heard her sing before that recording session didn't make her feel any better. Nor did Albert Grossman's telling her that because of her upper-class background she hadn't suffered enough to be a great singer. In just a few years, he would eat his words.

In the next four years, Carly worked at a number of jobs that neither interested nor stimulated her. But they were necessary, she says now, for their very unproductiveness. She was a secretary at *Newsweek* ("I loathed it. A tape recorder could have done what I was doing"); an incompetent production assistant; radio commercial writer for an ad agency whose clients included Bonnie Bell, a couple of banks, and Good 'n Fruity, candy cousin to Good 'n Plenty. She even taught guitar at a Berkshire music camp one summer, a job memorable only for meeting Jacob Brackman, with whom she later collaborated on a number of songs. She was very down on herself, getting fat, and getting fed up with not being able to find something that would make her happy.

"I think I felt a desire to break away from what my parents felt was important," Carly says about those years of groping. "For instance, my father was a book publisher, and I did my best never to read a book. It's just the old rebellious spirit.

"For a long time I was feeling that the only way I could get anyone's attention or love was by being the black sheep who wasn't making any money, didn't have a job, didn't fit in."

Carly let herself drift for almost five years, never really feeling comfortable with herself or her lack of direction. It was during this period that she started writing songs about her feelings, her highs and lows, her fears. She spent six months as the colead singer of Elephant's Memory, a "horn-rock" group, and it wasn't a particularly happy association. They wouldn't take her seriously, the way she wanted to be taken.

With Jacob Brackman, Carly kept on writing songs, and a record promoter—one of New York's biggest and best—Jerry Brandt, signed Carly up for his own production company, Brandtworks. She made a demo for him, and he took it over to Jac Holzman, then president of Elektra Records. He was impressed. Someone claimed Holzman was running around telling everyone he had found the female Mick Jagger, the first but certainly not the last time Carly was compared to him—musically as well as physically.

In 1971, she released her first solo album, *Carly Simon*. The single that came out of it, "That's The Way I've Always Heard It Should Be," was probably the most-played song of the year. It was, ironically, a song Carly had written when she was twenty-three or twenty-four and had first met Jacob Brackman. She was asked to write a theme song for a TV special, "Who Killed Lake Erie," and that's the melody she came up with. It was never used, and two years later, about six months before she recorded the album, Carly asked Jake, then a critic and essayist for *The New Yorker,* to write some lyrics for the tune. Carly had felt when they first met that their relationship would always be a special one and would be instrumental in her taking her first real step on her own. As it turned out, she was right. The song has become a classic, and their friendship is one they both treasure.

One of the reasons Jake and Carly had such an instant rapport was Jake's sensitivity to Carly as a person. Every song he has written has been one she identifies with, and even though "That's The Way" is a woman's song

—a disillusioned look at marriage—Jake's lyrics said exactly what Carly felt.

With a hit single and an album to her credit, Carly was ready to debut as a solo performer. Or as ready as she'd ever be. She was the opening act for Cat Stevens at Los Angeles's famous Troubadour on April 6, 1971, and she was absolutely terrified.

Not only was this her first show, but James Taylor, whom she greatly admired, was in the audience. They knew each other vaguely; both their families summered on Martha's Vineyard, and James had seen Carly perform with her sister Lucy in the early sixties. He is four years younger than Carly, and feeling that gap strongly when he was fourteen and she eighteen, he never even approached her then. But as he emerged as a fine and talented musician, Carly found herself being strongly influenced by his style—her lyrics, melodies, and playing all reflect this. She also was reminded, everytime he sang, of the carefree days on the Vineyard, a time near and dear to her.

She needn't have worried about that performance. She was unbeatable. The next few months saw her appearing in smallish clubs all over the country, like the Bitter End in New York. The reviews all around were superb: "an electric presence" one critic said; "wonderfully fascinating" another enthused. Even, and especially, James was impressed.

The man in her life at that moment was Kris Kristofferson. He was going through one of his heavy falling-asleep-at-the-microphone periods, and whenever they shared a bill, it was clearly Carly who was the dominant performer. Their relationship lasted a stormy six months, "with a five-month hiatus within that time," Carly jokes. Anyway, Carly and James were quietly getting to know each other.

Carly won a Grammy Award as the Best New Artist

of 1971, and she was firmly on the road to becoming one of the country's most popular singer/songwriters. But as exciting and rewarding as winning the Grammy was, it didn't begin to compare to the real big event of 1972.

In November, James Taylor and Carly Simon were married. Laughingly, they say they did it because "that's the way we always heard it should be," but actually it was Carly who suggested it and James who didn't think it was necessary at the time. He later decided it was the right thing to do at the moment. He announced it at the beginning of his concert at New York's Radio City Music Hall, and they celebrated at a 3:00 a.m. party in the Time-Life Building.

Shortly after the wedding, in early 1973, Carly released her second album, *Anticipation.* Later that year came *No Secrets* with the song that was to become Carly's biggest hit and the one she is most often identified with. "You're So Vain" was a challenge to the entire rock establishment. Who was that song about? Kris Kristofferson? Mick Jagger? James Taylor?

Mick Jagger seemed the likeliest candidate. He and Carly had been an item on and off for a few years, not to mention their remarkable physical resemblance. It was Mick who put Carly straight in terms of her music and where it should go—you're a rock singer, not a folk singer, he told her, and it changed her life. To top it off, Jagger sang the background vocals on the song. It looked like an open-and-shut case.

Carly met Mick when she thought she might like to try her hand at a journalism career. She offered to interview Mick for the "Arts and Leisure" section of the *Los Angeles Times,* and the *Times* accepted. She never did write the article, but interviewer and subject became good friends during the hours they spent talking. She didn't feel, after that, that she could be objective enough about him to write the story. Carly did expect, however, to see an immediate likeness between the two of them when they met. But if she had expected to walk into a mirror, she was disappointed. She thought they looked nothing alike.

When "You're So Vain" was released, tongues started wagging and the guessing games began. One dj in California even ran a contest for his listeners to write in and tell him who they thought the song was all about. But Carly, to this day, has never named names. She says, when asked, that "You're So Vain" is "really a little about anyone who suspects it may be about them. But the examples were really taken from my imagination. I had about two or three people in mind."

The song was written after she had already finished all the other songs for the album. She was a little tired of the self-pitying line her lyrics were taking, and she really wanted to come up with something more positive and more interesting than the things she had been dealing with.

"I didn't like to see myself talking about disenchantment as much as I had," she said. "The whole album was about things that never quite happened, things that didn't turn out the way I wanted them to, things that were disillusioning. 'You're So Vain' was kind of an accusative song that came out of my wanting to write something else."

The melody was one that Carly had written some time earlier, and the original lyrics were about a man named Ben who happened into her life at just the right time. She decided it was too gloomy and scratched the words, all except one line: "You're so vain, you probably think this song is about you."

Despite the fact that sales on both the single and the album were better than just good—they were fantastic— 1973 turned out to be a less than perfect year for Carly musically. Elektra Records was going through some heavy changes that affected her personally. Her mentor, Jac Holzman, left; Elektra merged with Asylum

Records, and Asylum's president, David Geffen, took over the combined company. There was much confusion, and Carly felt left out. The new management didn't know her and didn't seem to want to; they had their own stars to promote. Carly was particularly upset when her fourth album, *Hotcakes,* was released in January 1974 with a cluster of other records, including Bob Dylan's *Planet Waves* (his first for the label) and Joni Mitchell's *Court and Spark* (she was a Geffen protégée). She felt she should have been given more of the individual attention she had been promised and was angry enough to think about looking for a new label. Her personal manager, Arlyne Rothberg, talked her out of leaving and promoted or not, *Hotcakes* sold more than 1 million copies. There were two singles released from the album, "Haven't Got Time For The Pain" and "Mockingbird," the first recorded Simon/Taylor duet.

Hotcakes was written and recorded while Carly was pregnant with their first child, Sarah Maria, who was born on January 7, 1974. Carly was never happier, and the album shows it. The songs are up tempo and euphoric, and her voice is in exquisite shape.

It was around this time that James and Carly gave up their apartment in New York and moved to the Vineyard. James designed and built their country-style house, including a recording studio so they could both rehearse and record without leaving home. Carly was, as she puts it, into "nest building," spending most of her time taking care of Sarah and James and the house and trying to strike the right balance between her family and her career.

It was difficult for Carly to write just after Sarah was born; she has a strong domestic streak, and all her energies were put into caring for her child. It was not time Carly resented giving. In fact, those early, growing months with Sarah were ones she treasured more than anything else. And once she was no longer the baby's only contact with life, she did start writing again, the very kinds of songs inspired by the feelings she had when her body became her own again.

"After the whole maternal feeling of your body, and the feeling of being essential to someone else's life—and that is about as heavy as a woman could ever feel—after that passed, and my body began to assume its former shape, there was sort of a renewal. . . ."

With that renewal, though, came contradictions and confusions. Once you're a mother, Carly feels, you can't be a baby anymore; you can't be narcissistic, but you must give love. You have to think of a baby as an individual rather than as an extension of yourself, which is exactly what Carly tries to do with Sarah. But in the process, you give up a little something, and it hurts. Her next album, *Playing Possum*, was a sensual reflection of it all.

She says of the album in general, and of the particular song, "Slave," "It was more body than mind. I felt it more in my stomach than in my head while writing and performing it.

"It was dictated totally by what pleasured my ears. It was written very much for myself, rather than for any schooled knowledge of what I thought worked." She desperately wanted "Slave" to be the album's single, even though she knew there would be some fierce reaction to it from women who would take the lyrics at face value. It is not about being a slave to men, but about being angry at that state.

"The woman in 'Slave,'" Carly explains, "is watching herself having feelings of incompleteness—she realizes that no matter how far she's gone, there's still this undeniable dependence. Still, her ideals are to be whole by herself. The song is about her struggle to be free."

Elektra released "Attitude Dancing" as a single instead, with Carole King singing backup. It was a piece of puff, a catchy tune, advising "dance your own thing."

For all Carly's talk, the songs were about feelings, yes, but they seemed hardly as personal as her previous material. She more or less put herself into the role of storyteller, imagining the way things might be rather than reliving her own experiences. It was hard to put those kinds of things to music.

"I have trouble writing songs about James or Sarah," says Carly. "Or my married life. It seems so terribly, terribly personal to me. It seems so terribly private. There's a part of my life which I do not want to invade for the commercial market."

She has written several songs about James that will never be published. She writes to work out problems or to get things off her chest, and they are just too personal to ever be recorded. It is obvious, in so many of her lyrics, that she is talking about her life with her husband and the public aspect of their marriage. She once wanted all her songs about James to be positive until she realized that "you don't always have positive feelings about the person you live with."

James's songs, too, are autobiographical and revealing, and they both feel that if they were ever to release albums simultaneously, the world would know exactly what the current status of their relationship was. Carly is very carefully lightening up the tone of her songs so she doesn't give absolutely everything away. Even so, their current tranquility is more than just hinted at in her latest album, *Boys In The Trees.*

"I love being married to James, I really do," Carly says in one breath. In the next, she admits, "One minute I'm extolling the joys of being married to James, and the next hour I think how annoying it is to be married.

"People don't like to admit contradictions, but within them are challenges. Only recently have I become aware of how many parts there are to my life. And how they serve to confuse me."

Part of the confusion, for Carly at least, comes from

the traditional view that the man has to be the more dominant personality, especially if they are working in the same field. She admits there's great insecurity and anger on both their parts if they happen to have albums out at the same time and one is doing better than the other.

"We're jealous of each other and proud of each other at the same time," Carly says. "It's more comfortable if James is more successful than I am. Where we run into problems and where I start complaining about being used and abused comes from my own willingness to be subservient."

Carly knows that she is James's equal in all things, but there are times when she feels like "a slave to my own chauvinistic emotions." That's what "Slave" is all about, and she wrote it for all women who go through the same feelings.

The title of the album itself, *Playing Possum,* is Carly's stab at coming to terms with the life she leads. She had turned thirty, gotten married, had a child, and the idealism and radicalism that had shaped her earlier years had been replaced with domestic tranquility and professional satisfaction. Had she dropped out, or was she just on the brink of new changes, merely playing possum?

Coming to terms with this way of life was not necessarily an easy trip. Carly had to learn somewhere along the way to toughen herself up a bit, to say no to people even if it meant they might think she was not nice. She used to welcome everyone who came to their Vineyard door into the house; now she welcomes the privacy it affords. The Taylors will often make dinner reservations for themselves under a false name, and they avoid the trappings of superstardom like the plague.

Their house is modest, and Carly shuddered (but paid) at the cost of renting a house in Los Angeles while she was recording *Possum* (a mere $3,750 a month; previous tenants had been Liz Taylor, Mick Jagger and Sonny Bono). James is not a glamour boy—he owns, according to his wife, two suits, five pairs of pants, and never wears socks that match. Carly, on the other hand, doesn't feel guilt about buying an expensive dress or a $135 silk blouse, but she doesn't care if she doesn't either.

The kind of marriage the Taylors have takes them back and forth between the idyllic country/beach life of the Vineyard, where they are accorded no special privileges by their neighbors, and the New York/Hollywood hustle for recording dates and appearances. Whether she is on either coast, Carly worries about both of their positions on the charts as well as about clothes and makeup, although she'd rather not. They are trying very hard not to be known as either the Sonny and Cher or the Ozzie and Harriet of the rock world, but occasionally the shoes do fit.

Carly and James were offered the starring roles in *A Star Is Born* when the Joan Didion-John Gregory Dunne script was still alive, but the story was too close and at the same time not close enough. James did not have an alcohol problem. Yet their marriage did get off to a rocky start. He was remote and undependable, and there was a wall up between them that even love couldn't break down.

"It was a hard time because he wasn't easy to live with," Carly confesses. "Anyway, the beginning of our marriage went through a lot of pain. But, I suppose, if you start from that position, it has to work its way up."

Carly thinks her husband is a "genius" and "closer to being a real artist than anyone I know." Her own talent she sees as "sparks." They work at keeping their musical identities separate—they started out as individuals and just because they are married to one another doesn't mean they have to become one another. They'll back each other on vocals, like "Mockingbird," and they've written one song together, "Forever My Love," on *Hotcakes*. They'd like to write more, but there's a wide gap to bridge from husband and wife to collaborators in music. It's a world they're not quite into yet, although it will happen eventually.

Interestingly, Carly feels that marriage has changed her role in life, that it has not taken away any of her independence, but has in fact, given her even more.

"It's not the kind of independence that makes me free to fly off to Rio," she explains, "but I'm freer to know myself, which is the most important kind of freedom. I've gotten a certain amount of stability and self-assurance within a particular relationship that makes me open up to getting to know myself."

James agrees wholeheartedly. He thinks that while there are some real differences between men and women, as well as some culturally imposed ones, it's no longer a man's world, controlled by a man's outlook. And because of this change, he'd rather see Carly working and performing than behind the kitchen stove. Women who live vicariously through their husbands wind up making everyone crazy, he believes, and he can handle any competitive feelings by talking them out with his wife. He is not afraid that expressing his ideas about her work will chase her away.

"Carly and I are in love with each other," James says. "But love is not a thing you can find; it's an accumulated emotion in any one person, and love always has strings attached.

"When I love someone, I remember that love has hurt me and passed. When Carly loves me, she remembers that in order to get love she has had to do things she resented doing."

They manage to completely understand each other and play on their own mutual strengths, one of which, they both agree, is being in the same business. It helps them stay Carly Simon and James Taylor instead of melting into an amalgam of both.

To be Carly Simon is to be many things. To James she is person, woman, wife, lover, supporter, friend, confidant, artist. To Sarah, and the Taylors' younger child, Ben (born in January 1977), she is, of course, "mommy." To her fans, she radiates a long-legged sophistication that is offset by a flashy, full-bodied voice that contrasts strikingly with tender, lovely lyrics and tunes.

To herself, Carly has always been sort of the ugly duckling, too tall (she's 5'9"), big-boned, with features that "collide, run into each other." She's never quite all put together; "a mess," she says, "an overgrown waif." Her friends say that it's not a put on, that that's the real Carly for you. She says she doesn't have one particular image of herself, although other people do.

"I think people see me as a new kind of woman, very strong, very, very liberated, independent, large, forceful, big smile, big teeth.

"But I never think of myself as just one person. A lot of times I can be very shy—tremendously introverted and acquiescent and intimidated. At other times I can be the master of ceremonies . . . different people bring out different things in me."

She's never consciously tried to unify all those different aspects of herself either. It's far more interesting to just flow along with how you feel, and that's the way she tends to take it. Loose and easy.

The one part of herself that Carly does consciously try to control is her feeling of insecurity. She used to agree with people who didn't like her lyrics or her voice, because being liked was that important to her. Now, she's much more confident about what she's doing and even has an unkind word or two to say about the critics who are picking on her songs because they're happy ones. There's no law that says you have to be miserable or pay for your happiness to write good music, which was the theme of "Misfits," her song from *Hotcakes*. It may be hip to be unhappy when you're young, but affectations like that should disappear with maturity.

"It really is true that I write a lot more if I'm sort of low because very often I do write songs out of the need to solve a problem," Carly admits. "But fortunately my dilemmas are not as self-torturing as before. I've accepted that I'm not altogether neurotic and down-trodden and a miserable creature. I'm happy about being happy. . . I'm not interested in wallowing in self-pity anymore."

Did that attitude show up in the next album after *Possum, Another Passenger?* Maybe, maybe not. Probably the best song on the album is "In Times When My Head," which deals with a relationship with a man during the most difficult of moments. It is typically Carly, a song about insecurities. "Waited So Long," on the other hand, is a song that perhaps does reflect her own ease with herself. The album itself is the most rock of any she's done; some critics feel that it's her best yet, that she was finally able to leave her husband and child at home and write, perceptively and clearly, about other things.

It goes back to her attempt to simplify her music. She followed this album up with a single that she didn't write at all, Marvin Hamlisch's and Carole Bayer-Sager's "Nobody Does It Better," the theme song from the James Bond flick, *The Spy Who Loved Me*. It was hardly her usual cooing love song, but it sold as well as if it had been. She also cowrote a song for the Doobie Brothers and coproduced and wrote several songs for a friend, Libby Titus. She claims that writing for someone else is a "totally liberating experience," and she's no longer interested in making any statements. Her writing *is* getting looser, and she recently set herself up in an office on Central Park West to hasten the process along.

James and Carly now divide their time between the Vineyard and New York. It's not unusual to see the Taylors in Central Park or strolling down Broadway, just enjoying the city. Carly thinks she will always be drawn to the hustle and bustle of New York. After all, she was born there; her family and friends and her music are rooted in the city too.

"When I was growing up," she says, "I listened to a lot of show music, jazz, and classical music. My roots weren't country or black; they were eclectic. I think now my music is becoming less sophisticated; I'm starting to simplify."

Carly doesn't sit down each day at the same time and write songs. She's tried that, but besides being undisciplined and having a family to look after, she gets her ideas at all times. She has a book that she writes things down in as they happen, in conversations, experiences, or just while walking down the street. She calls it "stealing," taking her inspiration for her songs from catching the key phrases in a dialogue, listening to what other people say, eavesdropping. Just sitting down and trying to think up a song idea is not a fruitful way of working for her.

There isn't a true pattern in her writing, either, of music or lyrics first. If she's sitting at the piano or picking on the guitar, she might come up with a melody that has no words. And melody is more important to her than any other part of a song. Of course, tempo and rhythm are given their due, and sometimes she might lighten up a little on an involved or complicated melody to make a song rock. She works hard on each and every piece of music she writes.

"I'll get a melody and that will bring me back to the piano several times to perfect it. Then I'll write something else because I'm tired of playing the same thing so much. It's as it happens. Lyrics rarely happen at the same time, except for "Anticipation" for which I wrote the melody and the lyrics simultaneously."

Sometimes Carly will just have a stanza of lyrics, take

these lyrics over to the piano, and write the music around them. Then that is the inspiration for the next verse of lyrics. She tends to write most just before she has to put an album together, but she always has that book of ideas at the ready. Something as simple as seeing people in a restaurant who remind her of "aged royalty" is written down, and maybe becomes the basis for a song later or part of another one. She has the ear of a novelist and listens to people with the same kind of intensity. She once dated a writer who made her feel that everything she said was up for grabs; now she sort of does the same thing with others.

Whether she writes on the guitar or the piano makes a big difference in the way her songs turn out. She plays them both equally well, but the piano is a more familiar instrument, a more logical one from her point of view. She is comfortable with the chord progressions on the piano but is still unused to the way the guitar goes.

Carly's albums always sell well and so have several hit singles. In addition, she cares about sales—she wouldn't be a pop singer if she didn't.

She only releases, on the average, about one album a year. She doesn't believe in just churning things out like a machine. Her songs all have a very specific focus to them and reflect a side of life, she hopes, that hasn't been shown before. She tries, very consciously, to put a little bit of what is "definitely me" into each song without making them so personal that other people can't identify with them. They used to be like events from her personal diary, but that made them too close, and she couldn't get any persepective. Mel Brooks once told her that the reason she was so great was that she says things that are obvious, but no one else thinks to say them. That's Carly in a nutshell.

"I don't write a song unless I have a particular slant on something that I feel is unique," she says. "I'm not interested in writing anything unless it's going to stick out, unless it's a new way to express emotion. It's got to interest me in order for me to have the energy to write about it."

Strangely enough, it's that very uniqueness that everyone identifies with. It may be Carly's particular slant, but it exquisitely captures the feelings of her fans.

Even so, according to her brother, Peter, whom Carly considers her harshest critic, she's never quite sure when she puts out an album whether it's really good or not. She likes the people closest to her to tell her it's good, to tell her not to worry. She takes every bit of criticism very seriously, despite the fact that she's aware that rock critics are rather unpredictable people who can often be as cruel and unrelenting in their criticism as they can be flowery and effusive in their praise. She also has little patience with those people whom she thinks are just fair weather friends—the ones who are there when you're on top but do a fast disappearing act when things are at an ebb. It's a common enough phenomenon in the entertainment industry, and Carly's continuing popularity with the people who buy her records is certainly proof enough of her talent and her success.

Carly is an exception to one of the most hard-and-fast rules of the music industry—that to sell records you have to make personal appearances. That she's sold well over 7 million records in the past seven years, while her concert appearances have been limited to an occasional duet with James during one of his dates, is truly an unusual occurrence. She came out of her retirement in the summer of 1977 and played Greenwich Village's Other End to packed houses, and then took off with James on his tour. Later, she made an appearance on behalf of Brenda Feigen Fasteau, a candidate in the New York senate race, and then, finally, in May, she started a long overdue tour of her own. She loves to perform, but she needs the intimacy of small audiences so she can see their faces, relate to them personally, see whether they like her or not.

Everytime she gets up on a stage she feels as if she's transferring her old fears that her parents wouldn't love her if she didn't perform to her audience. Her parents' love was essential to her survival as a child; her audience's love is essential to her survival as an adult. It gives an audience an importance they are not really aware of, and the performer expects things of them that they cannot possibly fulfill. Carly has been trying to get to that point in her performing where she can get up and get into what she's doing without being aware of how many people are out there watching; she wants to become so totally unself-conscious that each performance automatically turns out to be as good as the one before it. The fear of rejection is a difficult one for her to overcome, and she's tried every self-help and therapeutic discipline around—hypnosis, yoga, analysis, books that promise to turn "anxiety into creativity"—and she's still scared.

Even at the Other End last summer, when the audience was packed with friends and family as well as fans, she admitted to terror before all her performances and on and off during them. She was pleased with the way they turned out, but sometimes the energy of an audience tends to overwhelm her, a feeling she doesn't at all like. Instead of being able to slough it off or even absorb all that energy and channel it into her music, which would be healthiest, she internalizes it, and it gets terribly confusing.

But she is getting better. She's up to facing it head-on as her ambitious, for her, 1978 tour schedule proved. The main reason she did it, besides promoting the new album, was to overcome her fears. She especially looked forward to the opening concert at the Bottom Line, just because New York audiences have a reputation for being especially hard to please. They weren't. The two nights at the Bottom Line were sold out long before the actual date. And Carly, as always, was absolutely super.

Her fantasy is being able to appear in small clubs under an alias so she could just sing her head off and nobody would expect too much from her or, conversely, hope that she fell flat on her face. As Frau Himmel, which is what James calls her, she could go from club to club, moving on as soon as anybody recognized her and getting immense satisfaction out of not having to live up to anyone's preconceptions of her.

"I would like to sort of be a gypsy," she muses, "roaming around with James and Sarah and Ben from town to town, playing these small clubs. Another fantasy we have is touring the world by boat. Taking musicians with us and maybe an eight-track machine. Touring the world, playing harbors. We'd like to do a lot of traveling before the kids get to be of school age."

For now, Carly's concentrating on some more practical arrangements, like the small clubs and auditoriums she's been booked into. The informality of that kind of setting puts her totally at ease. It's a paradoxical situation for Ms. Simon. Half of her is scared to death by the thought of success; the other half loves the excitement and the idea of having people move and respond to her music. She is, onstage—whatever she's feeling at the moment— electrifying. She looks confident, graceful, and has a magnetic personality. She is certainly not timid and afraid. Her voice is strong and rich; her songs are *her* songs.

When she can make eye contact with the audience, exchange currents with them—when they can't contain themselves and are standing up and applauding halfway through a song—she's more than okay, she is fantastic. And yet, she just can't let herself get, as she puts it, "flat-out stone excited" about success. It means to her that if she's got it, someone else hasn't, or maybe she just doesn't deserve it and will have to pay for it in some terrible way. It does bother her, and she'd like to be able to have the choice of wanting to perform or not perform on grounds other than just plain old fear. It's coming to that.

"It's such a paradox that it's become interesting to me," she says. "Instead of being afraid, I can look at myself as almost another person and I can think, 'Now, what is there to be afraid of in the first place?' " She feels so good about what she's doing that she can say confidently, "There are so many things I like about performing that I have tried to forget the things I don't like."

Two things Carly has most definitely gotten straightened out over the years is her relationship with her family and with the producer of most of her records, Richard Perry.

Commercially, Carly must be regarded as the most successful of the three Simon sisters. Joanna is more or less outside the realm of competition. As an opera singer, her renown in the musical community is unique, and being introduced as "Carly Simon's older sister" doesn't bother her in the least. Admittedly, she'd much rather have Carly introduced as her younger sister, but it really doesn't matter. Carly doesn't much like opera, though she respects Joanna's accomplishments and is proud and delighted with her success. Joanna, however, loves rock music and even volunteered to add a few oohs and ahhs to some of Carly's songs on *No Secrets*.

Lucy Simon has started recording again, and that's given her some very real problems. It is, in a way, unfortunate that her last name is Simon; the comparisons are inevitable, and Carly is a tough act to follow.

"When I was first trying to get a recording contract," Lucy says, "the contract always centered around my being Carly's sister. They all seemed to want me to be very closely identified with Carly, to make sure she'd sing on my albums, to have her producer produce my albums, that sort of thing. Carly was always the issue. I was very much on my guard then about being Carly's sister."

The guard came down after her first two albums held up on their own merit. She has been recognized as her own person by the critics and is hoping the public will do the same. "Just as a parent can love more than one child," she says, "I think there is enough room in the music world for many performers, even if they're in the same family."

Carly's glad for Lucy and certainly doesn't feel as if she's won any kind of contest to see who could make it biggest in the Simon family. She chooses to believe, instead, that the audiences and the races are different. The kind of help she's offered Lucy has been more in the nature of "goodwill and positive feelings"; support and a ready shoulder, rather than advice and a voice. They are friends as well as family, and there's a great deal of mutual admiration among the Simon Sisters.

Peter Simon, being the lone boy and the youngest member of the clan, has a very special relationship with Carly. She's his closest sister, and it's always been that way.

"She's a beautiful person, and I love her a lot," Peter says. "I guess she's always thought of me as the family hippie. She thought it was really far-out and beautiful— but it wasn't her kind of lifestyle."

Peter is a free-lance photographer with two books of pictures to his credit, *Moving On, Holding Still* and *Decent Exposure.* He planned a photo essay book on Carly, from childhood to marriage, with lots of family photos from his own personal collection. It's still in the making.

James Taylor comes from a performing family too. His brother Livingston has not enjoyed the same kind of success he has. Carly thinks their music sounds too much alike, and when their albums were released at the same time, it was a bit of overkill. James's sister, Kate, has an advantage in that she is female and different enough from her brothers to make more of an individual splash in the industry.

James and Carly share a similar attitude toward their respective families and the influences they had on their compulsion to perform. Both of them felt that performing was the only way to get attention—James, to win his mother's love away from his father; Carly to make herself noticed.

For James, being successful was a double-edged sword. Like Carly, he always felt that if he got what he wanted, he would, in some way, have to pay for it.

"Being successful might have carried with it an inherent anger at my mother or father for their wanting me to perform, their wanting me to do well," he explains. "Therefore, if I'm successful, there's an element of having done it for them and not having wanted to do it at all."

Carly feels that pressure was put on her at an early age to stand out, "not to be what I felt like being, which was, I guess, somewhere middle of the road. It had to be some kind of performance."

Her father was a particularly strong influence on her. "He was an utter narcissist," she remembers, "and he had a complete disregard for reality. I loved that. He believed he was special and that his children were special." He is present in a lot of Carly's lyrics, sometimes even subconsciously. When he died, Carly was fearfully angry with him and felt totally abandoned. It surfaced, years later, in a song called "Embrace Me, You Child," in which she pictures her dad as a rather frightening man.

Carly has gone through several producers on her albums, which is not unusual for a singer. But Richard Perry has produced four out of the eight, plus her hit single from *The Spy Who Loved Me*. She resisted working with him at first, feeling that his slick, commercial success with stars like Barbra Streisand, Ringo Starr, and Martha Reeves was not compatible with her own folksier style. But he was good for her; he pushed her in a direction she would herself have held back from, because he believed, along with Mick Jagger, that she was truly a rock singer.

"He's like a movie director," says Carly. "He sees himself holding the camera, directing the players, as doing a theme rather than as an interpreter." Carly didn't feel she needed that kind of producer since she wanted to call the shots herself. There was, often, a battle of wills, and Perry was not the producer on *Another Passenger*. Ted Templeman, who's produced Linda Ronstadt among others, was. But Carly admits that Richard Perry was often the reason some things she did were just good, while others were very good. He pushed them over the line.

"Richard was more of a producer than I've ever had before. He really was a hundred percent there, and even though I had to fight with him about a lot of tunes, he is the strongest producer I've known, and his personality goes right into all his records."

It was to Richard that Carly went with her songs for *Boys In The Trees*. They were almost all love songs.

"You're coming from a different place, from your heart, not your head," he told her enthusiastically. She had toned down the cerebral aspects of her music, made them less like poetry and more like lyrics.

As with her melodies and her lyrics, Carly's style has mellowed over the years. There have been many influences on her music, and early on in her career, she decided that she didn't want to sound like any of the popular female vocalists around. So she listened to the male singers, learned from their phrasing, and developed her own way. James Taylor, of course, was one singer she listened to a lot. And Cat Stevens, to whom she dedicated *Anticipation*. "I wanted to get next to him in some way so badly that I did the Troubadour date with him," she remembers. It was her first solo, and whatever her reason, it was the right thing to do. Cat introduced her to the man who produced *Anticipation,* Paul Samwell-Smith, whom Carly says tapped a "fragility" in her that hasn't been seen much on her albums since.

She had always admired Mick Jagger's style as well and doesn't deny his position in her own development. The only thing she does deny is all those past reports of her romances with him and the male stars she's worked with. She really never did get to know a lot of the people she was thrown together with on double-bills, and those "relationships" were products of imaginative minds and Carly's own problems figuring out whether her costars were more admirable as musicians or people.

One of the real relationships was with Kris Kristofferson, who always made her feel as if he might toss her out any minute. If nothing else, it made her write.

People have influenced Carly in many ways. She credits her brother Peter and her friend Jake as being two of the most important.

"Meeting Jake was an auspicious event that changed my life because he changed my thinking about myself and also brought me into contact with many people who are now my friends," Carly is happy to say.

"Jake was like a brother I never met until I was twenty-three, and Peter, my real brother, has been one of my closest friends, a person I can rely on for the truth, even though I don't want it sometimes."

And Arlyne Rothberg, her manager, has been as much of a friend to Carly as an adviser. She's very sensitive to Carly's needs and doesn't push her into the kinds of deals that would definitely make money but would probably destroy her client in the process.

Two musicians, guitarist Jimmy Ryan and drummer

Russel Kunkel, are also credited by Carly as having been particularly important to her. Jimmy encouraged her to play the Troubadour that first time and was right there by her side to help her out if anything went wrong. Russel played the drums for Carly during that appearance and made her feel so sure of herself that she calls him her "saint." If these two hadn't been there for Carly, she might never have played that gig and never have been formally introduced to James.

And if Carly had never met James. . .

But things are never quite that cut-and-dried, and neither is Carly Simon Taylor. She's a complex being, confident and talented, yet still shy of displaying it to others; a dedicated career woman who will always put her family first; an insightful and perceptive songwriter who can still bring a touch of wide-eyed innocence to her sophisticated music. It's been a long, hard grind to get to this point, where all the elements of her life are nicely falling into place, and the sacrifices and the doubts are minimal.

No one ever said life was easy, but for Carly and James that's what keeps it interesting.

DISCOGRAPHY

Carly Simon   *Carly Simon*, Elektra
Anticipation, Elektra
No Secrets, Elektra, EKS-75049
Hotcakes, Elektra 7E-1002
Playing Possum, Elektra 7E-1033
Another Passenger, Elektra
Boys In The Trees, Elektra

The MS READ-a-thon needs young readers!

Boys and girls between 6 and 14 can join the MS READ-a-thon and help find a cure for Multiple Sclerosis by reading books. And they get two rewards — the enjoyment of reading, and the great feeling that comes from helping others.

Parents and educators: For complete information call your local MS chapter, or call toll-free (800) 243-6000. Or mail the coupon below.

Kids can help, too!